"*Gender Identity and Faith* deliv̲.̲.̲ ̲ ̲ ̲ ̲ ̲ ̲ ̲ ̲ ̲ ̲ ̲ ̲ g with individuals seeking therapy to better understand ana integrate ̲ ̲ ̲ ̲ of their identity related to gender and religion/spirituality. Yarhouse and Sadusky provide specific interventions that can be used with clients, accompanied by numerous case examples to illustrate how to approach this complex topic with nuance and cultural humility. Given that many clients seeking therapy for gender-related needs also have a faith background that impacts their sense of self, this book is an essential read for all mental health providers working with gender diverse and transgender individuals."

Laura Edwards-Leeper, chair of the child and adolescent committee of the World Professional Association for Transgender Health and member of the child and adolescent groups revising the standards of care for transgender persons

"Too often, we who counsel and coach other persons erroneously believe our job is to offer solutions to the complex overlap of philosophy, religion, and gender identity. Using multiple worksheets, *Gender Identity and Faith* greatly helps religious and non-religious counselors and coaches to come alongside the transgender-presenting client and, by offering questions, to assist the client in exploring their amazing inner worlds."

Caryn LeMur, a male-to-female transsexual and a follower of the words and life of Jesus

"The authors' considerable experience is informed by a deep and thorough knowledge of the psychology, biology, culture, and politics needed to protect the transgender individual. Although certainly a valuable resource for practitioners who work with conventionally religious families navigating gender identity and faith, this book is also wonderfully accessible to all."

Tamara Pryor, adjunct associate professor of psychiatry at the University of Kansas School of Medicine-Wichita and executive director of clinical and research at EDCare

"*Gender Identity and Faith* represents a sophisticated and highly competent approach to engaging a clinical niche rarely addressed with either sophistication or competence in all areas: clinical practice around the intersection of gender identity and religious concerns. The common impulse in this area is either to prioritize one area over the other (either religion or gender identity). The authors embrace an alternative client-centered approach. The text offers a practical outline of their treatment model with clear and persuasive rationales. This is not a polemical text aimed to fight in the gender identity culture wars or at presenting a theology of gender or gender identity. It is a standout resource text for Christian clinicians and other professionals who are attempting to help clients well navigate issues of personal religious faith and gender identity. It represents a best-practices example of Christian clinical and role integration in the mental health fields and is illustrated with rich case studies."

William L. Hathaway, executive vice president for academic affairs at Regent University and professor in and former dean of the School of Psychology and Counseling at Regent

"If you serve clients seeking to honor both their deep personal faith and their gender identity questions, you'll find robust concepts and practical tools in this resource. You'll boost your competency with flexible assessments, worksheets, strategies, and case studies to help clients of all ages navigate culturally sensitive and spiritually profound questions of gender identity."

Pieter Valk, licensed professional counselor and director of EQUIP

GENDER
IDENTITY
& FAITH

Clinical Postures, Tools, and Case Studies
for Client-Centered Care

MARK A. YARHOUSE &
JULIA A. SADUSKY

Academic

An imprint of InterVarsity Press
Downers Grove, Illinois

InterVarsity Press
P.O. Box 1400, Downers Grove, IL 60515-1426
ivpress.com
email@ivpress.com

InterVarsity Press® is the book-publishing division of InterVarsity Christian Fellowship/USA®, a movement of students and faculty active on campus at hundreds of universities, colleges, and schools of nursing in the United States of America, and a member movement of the International Fellowship of Evangelical Students. For information about local and regional activities, visit intervarsity.org.

All Scripture quotations, unless otherwise indicated, are taken from The Holy Bible, New International Version®, NIV®. Copyright © 1973, 1978, 1984, 2011 by Biblica, Inc.™ Used by permission of Zondervan. All rights reserved worldwide. www.zondervan.com. The "NIV" and "New International Version" are trademarks registered in the United States Patent and Trademark Office by Biblica, Inc.™

While any stories in this book are true, some names and identifying information may have been changed to protect the privacy of individuals.

Figure 4.3: scaffolding image: Didgeman / 2403 images / Pixabay
Figure 9.1 Taken from Understanding Gender Dysphoria by Mark A. Yarhouse. © 2015 by Mark A. Yarhouse. Used by permission of InterVarsity Press, P.O. Box 1400, Downers Grove, IL 60515, USA. www.ivpress.com
Figure 9.2 Taken from Understanding Gender Dysphoria by Mark A. Yarhouse. © 2015 by Mark A. Yarhouse. Used by permission of InterVarsity Press, P.O. Box 1400, Downers Grove, IL 60515, USA. www.ivpress.com

The publisher cannot verify the accuracy or functionality of website URLs used in this book beyond the date of publication.

Cover design and image composite: David Fassett
Interior design: Jeanna Wiggins
Images: Green leaves on white background: © Eugene Golovesov / Pexels.com
*   Silhouette of a human: © neoncat / iStock / Getty Images Plus*
*   Abstract marble waves: © oxygen / Moment / Getty Images*

ISBN 978-0-8308-4181-3 (print)
ISBN 978-0-8308-4182-0 (digital)

Printed in the United States of America ⊗

InterVarsity Press is committed to ecological stewardship and to the conservation of natural resources in all our operations. This book was printed using sustainably sourced paper.

Library of Congress Cataloging-in-Publication Data
Names: Yarhouse, Mark A., 1968- author. | Sadusky, Julia, author.
Title: Gender identity and faith : clinical postures, tools, and case studies for client-centered care / Mark A.
*   Yarhouse and Julia A. Sadusky.*
Description: Downers Grove, IL : InterVarsity Press, [2022] | Series: Christian association for psychological studies
*   books | Includes bibliographical references and index.*
Identifiers: LCCN 2021053197 (print) | LCCN 2021053198 (ebook) | ISBN 9780830841813 (print) | ISBN
*   9780830841820 (digital)*
Subjects: LCSH: Gender identity—Religious aspects—Christianity. | Gender identity disorders. | Church work.
Classification: LCC BT708 .Y368 2022 (print) | LCC BT708 (ebook) | DDC 241/.664—dc23/eng/20211130
LC record available at https://lccn.loc.gov/2021053197
LC ebook record available at https://lccn.loc.gov/2021053198

P	25	24	23	22	21	20	19	18	17	16	15	14	13	12	11	10	9	8	7	6	5	4	3	2	1
Y	43	42	41	40	39	38	37	36	35	34	33	32	31	30	29	28	27	26	25	24	23	22			

CONTENTS

PART 4: CASE STUDIES

PREFACE

As we wrote this book, Arkansas became the first state to limit certain medical interventions—puberty blockers, hormone therapy, and gender-confirmation surgery (formerly called sex-reassignment surgery)—for minors (Cox, 2021). Many lesbian, gay, bisexual, transgender, queer, and other (LGBTQ+) interest groups have actively opposed this legislation, framing it as "anti-LGBTQ+" in its potential consequences for young people who are navigating gender identity or who represent a diverse gender identity.

According to a recent *USA Today* report, fifteen other states are considering similar legislation. The South Carolina bill under consideration, for example, would apply to any youth under age eighteen. This bill proposes to limit "gender reassignment medical treatment," which it defines as the following health care interventions:

(a) interventions to suppress the development of endogenous secondary sex characteristics;

(b) interventions to align the patient's appearance or physical body with the patient's gender identity; and

(c) interventions to alleviate symptoms of clinically significant distress resulting from gender dysphoria, as defined in the Diagnostic and Statistical Manual of Mental Disorders, 5th Edition.[1]

Depending on which version of the legislation is adopted, professional and legal consequences could ensue for medical professionals who provide

---

[1] Youth gender reassignment prevention act, SC H.4716 (2020) 123d session of General Assembly, www.scstatehouse.gov/sess123_2019-2020/bills/4716.htm. Although not an identical set of concerns, parents in the United Kingdom brought a complaint against the Tavistock Clinic in which it was suggested that minors are not receiving sufficient assessment and care as they present with gender-identity concerns. See Doward (2018).

these interventions to minors (Lamb, 2020). Consequences could include professional discipline, loss of one's license, fines, a charge of malpractice, and even a felony conviction. LGBTQ+ groups have responded by insisting that the medical coverage and care of transgender youth must be protected.[2]

While legislation like that passed in Arkansas and comparable bills being considered in South Carolina are at odds with the efforts of LGBTQ+ groups, other recent public policy decisions reflect the impact of LGBTQ+ advocacy. Legislation limiting gender-identity-change efforts (GICE) has been passed in as many as nineteen states and will likely continue to be introduced in other states. For example, New York's legislation on sexual-orientation-change efforts (SOCE) also includes restrictions on "efforts to change behaviors, gender identity, or gender expressions."[3] New York's legislation also clarifies that the limits it places on SOCE "shall not include counseling for a person seeking to transition from one gender to another."

Like the anti-medical-transition legislation adopted in Arkansas and proposed in South Carolina and other states, this anti-GICE legislation also includes professional and legal consequences for those who violate restrictions. However, these consequences threaten a very different group of medical practitioners.

We do not intend by this brief glimpse of the landscape to imply that these two sets of legislation are equivalent. The major mental health professional organizations in the United States have weighed in on these discussions and are against SOCE and GICE. They have also weighed in against efforts to limit access to medical services that would support and facilitate transition.

The reason we cite these divergent perspectives is to underscore that we are at a cultural moment in which the care provided to minors who are navigating questions around their gender identity is under great scrutiny, frequently polarized, and hotly contested. When legislation is introduced on either side of these debates, it may be well intended, but it can have a chilling effect on actual practice, limiting who is willing to work with people navigating gender-identity questions.

---

[2]It is widely believed that the South Carolina bill and others like it were introduced in response to a high-profile custody battle that included a dispute over care for a minor navigating gender identity. See Zraick (2019).

[3]An act to amend the education law, in relation to prohibiting sexual orientation change efforts by mental health providers, NY S04917-B (2013), https://legislation.nysenate.gov/pdf/bills/2013/S4917B

This book, then, is a timely resource for clinicians and others looking to gain awareness of the cultural, ideological, and political polarization surrounding care for young people navigating gender-identity questions. However, opinions and recommendations in this area are changing rapidly. We want to acknowledge that standards of care are subject to change over time, and no one book can possibly account for these possible changes in their totality. At the time of writing this, the World Professional Association for Transgender Health (WPATH) 2011 standards are in place, and these will inform our approach (Coleman et al., 2012). We recognize that changes in WPATH guidelines and updated research ought to lead to adjustments in conceptualization and treatment approaches. We are eager to learn alongside the field and will incorporate new information as it comes, knowing full well that we cannot fully predict and account for those updates here.

With that caveat in mind, the approach taken in this book reflects years of clinical experience that became more formalized after a special panel convened by the American Psychological Association (APA) to provide recommendations to the Substance Abuse and Mental Health Services Administration (SAMHSA) on SOCE and GICE with minors. One of the panel's recommendations was to help youth explore their gender identity without a "fixed outcome" (SAMHSA, 2015). This proposal was meant to guard against two sets of concerns facing the consensus panel. In one direction, the panel wanted to caution against relying on gender stereotypes to discipline a child toward resolving gender conflicts with their natal sex. In the other direction, the panel was concerned about premature transitioning without sufficient gender-identity exploration or amelioration of coexisting mental health concerns.

Although many transgender-affirming resources are available today (and more will undoubtedly be made available in the years ahead), some of these approaches raise more questions than answers for conventionally religious families whose religious doctrines and values, including religious norms regarding sex and gender, inform their decision making.

As we were writing this resource, we were faced with the question of language and terminology usage for sex and gender. We want to take a moment to share with the reader our perspective on language, because how we discuss the topics and the terms used is important. We tend to use the term *natal sex* (or *natal male* or *natal female*) to refer to the sex of a person at the time of their birth, their biological sex, or what is now sometimes referred to as their sex assigned at birth or sex designated at birth. The latest version of the APA Publication Manual (7th ed.) recommends writers avoid terms such as *biological sex* or *natal sex* in favor of "sex assigned at birth" or "sex designated at birth."[4] The Publication Manual voices the concern that reference to *biological* or *natal sex* can be viewed as disparaging by some scholars in this area and by some members of the transgender community. These terms imply "that sex is an immutable characteristic without sociocultural influence." We want to be respectful and mindful of how different people may respond to different terms and model that in our writing as well.

Conventionally religious persons are a subset of the population who are more likely to view sex as an immutable characteristic (whereas gender may be more subject to sociocultural influences). We certainly need to be aware of how language may be experienced by different transgender and nonbinary persons and their support people and adapt language accordingly. Because this resource is for practitioners who work with conventionally religious families, we encourage clinicians to be thoughtful and nimble in their use of language with this population and to account for intersecting identities that ought to inform their language. As a result, we use mostly "natal sex" and at times "gender assumed at birth" in this book to reflect the challenges with language and terminology and to underscore for the reader the need to be flexible in working with conventionally religious families and children, adolescents, and adults who are navigating gender identity and faith. In this book, the language preference is context specific to illustrate the flexibility that may be helpful in responding respectfully to the person sitting in front of us, and if an individual is troubled by the use of a particular term, it can allow for robust dialogue among family members, growth in empathy, and adaptations in language when indicated.

Clinicians need a client-centered, open-ended approach to care that makes room for gender exploration while respecting conventional religiosity. Such an approach must be flexible enough to aid family members who perceive matters of gender identity and religious identity differently. It must provide clinicians with ways of thinking about gender identity and

---

[4]See Gender, in *APA Style* (last updated August 2021). https://apastyle.apa.org/style-grammar-guidelines/bias-free-language/gender

religion in order to help them serve families for whom these experiences are particularly salient.

This resource carves out clinical space for mental health professionals to help people who wish to take their gender identity seriously, to take their religious identity seriously, and to take the relationship between their gender identity and religious identity seriously. It is designed for practitioners working with clients who wish to explore their gender identity in ways that position them (and, in the case of minors, their parents) to pursue congruence between their gender identity and their faith.

ACKNOWLEDGMENTS

WE ARE UNABLE TO THANK BY NAME the countless members of the institute whose research informs our approach. We want to begin by acknowledging the work that went into our initial workbook, *Gender Identity Journeys*. With the help of Dr. Trista Carr and Dr. Emma Bucher, we developed this workbook to aid clients in the exploration of some aspects of their gender identity and faith. We also want to thank Caryn LeMur, who offered several suggestions, some of which were incorporated into that resource. The workbook was recently revised with the assistance of members of the Sexual and Gender Identity Institute, especially Chuck Cruise, whom we would also like to particularly thank for his contributions. Some of that material was initially presented in chapter six of *Understanding Gender Dysphoria* and was retained and expanded on here.

We could not have developed this present resource without the help of Dr. Gregory Coles, who offered careful assistance with editing and feedback early in the writing process. We also benefited from the feedback of several licensed psychologists, including Dr. Laura Edwards-Leeper, an internationally recognized expert on transgender and gender-diverse youth, and Dr. Diane Chen, Behavioral Health Director for The Potocsnak Family Division of Adolescent and Young Adult Medicine at the Ann & Robert H. Lurie Children's Hospital, both of whom offered wisdom and critique that have helped us develop this resource in its present form. Thanks also to Ethan Martin for his work on the index.

Above all else, we are forever grateful for the countless individuals, families, and couples we have met with who bravely shared their gender-identity journeys with us. Whenever a story is shared in this book, the names and some details have been changed to protect their anonymity. Their diverse experiences are each worth sharing, learning from, and taking seriously as we approach such complex and important clinical work.

ABBREVIATIONS

AAP	American Academy of Pediatrics
APA	American Psychological Association
ASD	autism spectrum disorder
DBT	dialectical behavior therapy
DSM	American Psychiatric Association, *Diagnostic and Statistical Manual of Mental Disorders*
GCS	gender-confirmation surgery
GICE	gender-identity-change efforts
GRIT	Gender and Religious Identity Therapy
HT	hormone therapy
LGBTQ+	lesbian, gay, bisexual, transgender, queer, and other
SAMHSA	Substance Abuse and Mental Health Services Administration
SOCE	sexual-orientation-change efforts
WPATH	World Professional Association for Transgender Health

PART 1

OVERVIEW OF GENDER IDENTITY IN THERAPY

1

RELIGIOUS IDENTITY
AND GENDER IDENTITY
IN THERAPY

Michael and Micaela are a married couple in their late thirties. They have a five-year-old child, Xavier, whose gender-atypical mannerisms and interests they describe as "different." They are Christians and concerned about the best way to respond to and support Xavier.

Dani is a twenty-one-year-old natal female who reports distress associated with her gender incongruence. She is asking for help navigating gender-identity concerns in light of her spiritual beliefs. She has been isolating from her church friends, who all volunteer at the youth group there, for fear of what they would think if they knew about her difficulties.

RJ is a fifty-five-year-old natal male who has been married for thirty years. He and his wife, Kathy, identify as Christians. RJ reports he has been wrestling with his gender identity throughout their marriage and before they were married, and now that their children are out of the house, he reports a pressing desire to transition to female.

Evie is a twenty-nine-year-old single mother of two. Her youngest, Chris, is ten years old. Chris has made a social transition at home and at the local elementary school. Evie has called the church office to inform the church that Chris will present as a girl in the fall and that she wants Chris to be able to participate in children's ministry accordingly.

Karen and Henry are a newly married couple in their late twenties. Henry has struggled with gender dysphoria since childhood, but the intensity of the dysphoria has ebbed and flowed, reaching its peak two years into their three-year marriage. The couple are high school sweethearts and the best of friends, but they are wrestling with the future of their marriage, given how distressing Henry's dysphoria has become and how much he longs for hormonal treatment. They believe marriage is a covenant, which makes it difficult to know where to go from here in light of their faith.

Matt and Lisa have four children, and their youngest, Jonah, just turned eight years old. They have noticed that Jonah frequently wears his older sister's dress clothes and asks Lisa when his hair will be long like hers. Jonah sometimes wakes up at night crying, saying, "I prayed that God would make me a girl, and he won't listen to me."

This book is addressed to mental health professionals with questions about providing services to conventionally religious clients whose gender identity does not correspond to their natal sex nor their gender assumed at birth. You may be reading it because, like many health care professionals, you have experienced a recent increase in referrals of such cases. The six cases with which we have opened this chapter reflect just a few of the many diverse gender presentations we have seen in our practices.

This book is not written to Christian counselors specifically; rather, it is intended for a broader audience of mental health professionals, including Christians, who find themselves working with individuals, couples, and families who are conventionally religious and whose religious faith is an important consideration in navigating gender-identity questions.

A book like this is important because the clinical and broader societal landscapes have become incredibly polarized around the very existence of transgender and other diverse gender identities. Disputes abound over the best way to care for people navigating gender identity and—in the case of this book—the intersection of gender identity and religious identity.

In this chapter we want to offer a snapshot of not only the kinds of cases we see in practice but also the current trends and controversies in care, as well as the general parameters of our approach. Note that several things distinguish our approach from existing approaches, including that (a) we do not focus on changing gender identity, and (b) we do offer concrete and specific strategies for exploring conflicts of gender identity and religious identity.

Our specialty is helping individuals, couples, and families who take their religious faith seriously, who take the questions they have about their gender identity seriously, and who take the relationship between their religious identity and gender identity seriously.

Of course, not everyone who comes to our offices asking for help is navigating gender identity and faith. Here are some of the other clients we have seen for a range of concerns:

- Shannon is a male-to-female transgender person who is asking for treatment for panic attacks that keep her from performing at her job.

- CJ is a natal male who is planning to transition in the next year. The decision has been made and is not up for discussion. CJ is asking for help crafting a letter to communicate this decision to adult children.

- Kris is a nineteen-year-old natal female who describes themselves as gender nonbinary and prefers they/them pronouns. Kris is requesting help with improving family relationships with their family, none of whom identifies as religious.

- Artie is an eighteen-year-old who just graduated high school and expresses interest in a social transition to female. Artie does not identify as religious and elects not to have religion be a part of the clinical services provided.

Some of our clients come to us simply asking for help addressing symptoms of depression, anxiety, or any number of other challenges. In these cases, the fact that the client is transgender is an important demographic variable, an individual characteristic, but gender identity is not directly significant to why the person is seeking clinical services. Other clients experience symptoms of depression or anxiety stemming from other people's responses to their gender-identity questions, including experiences of discrimination, microaggressions, family conflicts, or peer rejection. In other words, these clients may not themselves experience a conflict between their gender identity and faith, but they are navigating relationships that are important to them, and some of these relationships may have been strained due to the client's exploration of gender identity. We will touch on these kinds of relationships in this book, but they are secondary to our primary focus, which is to help individuals navigate religious-identity and gender-identity questions when such questions present tensions for them.

FOCUS OF THIS RESOURCE

The purpose of this book is to serve as a resource specifically to *clinicians who work with conventionally religious clients and families for whom religious dimensions appear to be in conflict with their gender-identity questions.* That is, the client (or, in some cases, the family) is navigating gender identity and faith identity and is asking for assistance in making sense of the relationship between these two salient aspects of experience. As we noted above, a secondary emphasis in this book is helping clients navigate relationships strained by differences in beliefs and values about gender identity and faith.

We have come to understand the great difficulties that can arise for those who pursue therapy to resolve such conflicts. Many individuals have come to us after pursuing therapy with other providers, having found these providers' techniques to be irrelevant or outright damaging. In some cases, a therapist has underappreciated the significance of the client's beliefs and values, encouraging them to leave behind their religious or spiritual convictions and questions in order to become a healthy and whole person. In other cases, a therapist has encouraged stereotypical gender roles in a way that increased feelings of shame and ultimately heightened the conflict the client felt. Still others have avoided therapists altogether, for fear that being known with regard to their gender identity would put them in so great a conflict with their sense of self, their faith community, or God that they cannot see a way forward.

THREE MEANING-MAKING STRUCTURES

Yarhouse's previous work (2015) introduced the idea that there are at least three meaning-making structures or explanatory frameworks that represent different ways people understand diverse gender identities. These frameworks function as lenses through which people see the topic of gender identity today. The three lenses are the *integrity* lens, the *disability* lens, and the *diversity* lens. These lenses can represent unique conflicts that may arise between religious identity and gender identity and have been helpful points of reference in consultations and counseling.

In our work with conventionally religious families, the *integrity* (or *sacred*) lens has been the primary lens through which at least some family members understand sex and gender. This lens is based on widely held, traditional understandings of male/female difference that reflect sex and gender norms.

The lens perceives certain inherent differences between how males and females ought to behave, what one theologian (Gagnon, 2007) refers to as an "essential maleness" and an "essential femaleness." To violate these categories of essence is, according to the integrity lens, to violate the ethics of gender.

The *disability* (or *departure*) lens views gender-atypical behavior as a departure from the norm. When a person experiences incongruence between their natal sex and gender identity—where the vast majority of people experience congruence—that person's incongruence represents a difference or variation from what is expected. Many people who adopt the disability lens believe this difference indicates that something is not functioning as it should. This lens does not imbue the lack of congruence with moral significance in the way that the integrity, or sacred, lens does. However, it still implies concern over the lack of congruence. This concern tends to manifest in empathy for the experience of incongruence, rather than seeing it as an ethical violation in need of correction.

The *diversity* lens is the lens depicted in most popular entertainment, media, and so on; it is the lens toward which much of Western culture is rapidly moving. This lens views gender incongruence not as a concern to be corrected (integrity) or as a condition to sympathize with (disability) but as a difference in experience that reflects a different kind of person. The diversity lens calls for more celebration of the variation among gender experiences and expressions. Some of the most vocal advocates of the diversity lens call for the deconstruction of sex and gender norms because these norms are sometimes considered oppressive.

We will talk in subsequent chapters about how best to think about and discuss these lenses when providing consultations or ongoing counseling services to individuals and families navigating gender identity. You can also discuss with clients ways in which they might draw on the strengths they see in different lenses to support an integrated lens of some kind. For now, we simply want you to be familiar with the lenses and begin to think through how each lens reflects different points of tension for people navigating gender identity and religious identity.

Regardless of people's past experiences of therapy, it is integral to appreciate the power of a safe therapeutic relationship for those navigating gender-identity concerns. They are at a particular intersection of conflict, where beliefs—whether their own or their family's—and lived experiences present a unique challenge to overcome. Integrating personhood and values is no easy feat, especially in our current cultural landscape. Those navigating this intersection are often misunderstood both by people who do not identify with a faith tradition and by people within their faith communities. They are in need of clinicians who can journey with them without a fixed outcome. Our hope is that this book can aid that process.

2

ASSESSMENT

IN THIS CHAPTER OUR GOAL is to help clinicians ask relevant questions to get an accurate account of their clients' religious beliefs and values, gender-identity development, and any conflict clients may experience between their religious and gender identities. We will distinguish between assessment of children and assessment of adolescents/adults since this is a common distinction in the literature.

CULTURAL HUMILITY & ASSESSMENT

As Hopwood and Witten (2017) remind mental health professionals, it is important that we clinicians become aware of our own beliefs and values and potential biases so that we are able to assess culture, beliefs, and values and incorporate multiple aspects of diversity, including religious and spiritual issues, in therapy in a respectful and competent manner. Our ethical obligation is to work actively to eliminate or significantly reduce the effects that biases can have on our work and to foster deep respect for the cultural and individual variables at play. In fact, practice guidelines explicitly discuss the influence of religion and spirituality on the decisions people make regarding gender identity, as well as access to resources, level of stress, resilience, and coping. This too offers a clear emphasis on taking seriously the intersection of cultural identities and exploring the "salience of these aspects of identity" in an ongoing way (American Psychological Association [APA], 2015, guideline 3).

Keep in mind that it is beyond the competencies of mental health professionals to adjudicate theological positions of major world religions or to prescribe a fixed way of integrating these positions into personal beliefs and values. Respect for the rights of individuals to self-determination is central to the mental health field. However, clinicians can speak to the mental health correlates of lives informed by or shaped by various teachings, as well as to some of the challenges in navigating gender identity and religious faith. Indeed, it is important to identify our own biases about religion as they arise. Clinicians will benefit from acknowledging that we cannot fully understand any individual's particular experience. Thus, clinicians do well to invite clients to correct us insofar as we misunderstand, misrepresent, or devalue their religious/spiritual beliefs and other aspects of culture for them or those of their family. This is an important starting point as we enter into assessment of religious identity, gender identity, and exploration of the intersection of these and other aspects of identity in those we meet with.

In our clinical work, we have found that many clients are wary of mental health professionals for fear of their beliefs and values or their own experiences of gender identity being villainized, pathologized, or otherwise disregarded. Rapport building is best accomplished when these tensions and concerns are addressed overtly as part of the assessment process; this goes far in highlighting the dedication to ethical care for those we serve. Honest rapport and mutual understanding in the assessment process is most likely in the context of building trust and a nonjudgmental openness to the particular and nuanced experiences of individual clients and families.

There are important nuances to consider when it comes to working with gender minorities across different racial and ethnic groups. The Williams Institute at UCLA reported that 0.6% of the adult population identify as transgender. They estimate that 0.8% are African American or Black, 0.8% are Latina/o or Hispanic, 0.5% are White, and 0.6% are of another race or ethnicity. Additionally, in the U.S. Transgender Survey, 62% of participants identified as White, 17% as Latina/o, 13% as Black, 5% as Asian, 3% as multiracial, less than 0.1% as Native American, and less than 0.1% as Middle Eastern (Flores et al., 2016, p. 7).[1] Of note, people of color "experience deeper and broader patterns of discrimination than white respondents and the U.S. population" as a whole, including increased likelihood of living in poverty, being unemployed, and living with HIV (James et al., 2016, p. 6). This further highlights the diversity among transgender people and the importance of attending to the intersection of various aspects of identity as they relate to

---

[1]The 2015 U.S. Transgender Survey, which is the largest survey examining the lives and experiences of transgender people in the United States, is available at www.ustranssurvey.org.

quality of life, risk factors and strengths, goals for therapy, and so on. Exploration of ethnic identity as well as its interaction with religious identity can also help us unearth both challenges and resilience factors for different individuals who come to therapy around gender identity, and we would be remiss if we didn't highlight this early on in the explanation of our approach.

ASSESSMENT OF RELIGIOUS IDENTITY

Most of the individuals and families who seek counseling from us at the intersection of gender identity and religious identity consider themselves highly religious. Understanding the precise nature of these religious beliefs and values is crucial to evaluating the conflict people may experience with their gender identity (or that of a loved one). Clinicians must assess religious identity, then, because a person's religious and spiritual beliefs will shape their response to their own gender experience or that of a loved one.

Psychologists have developed measures for many aspects of religion and spirituality in a person's life. Clinicians can consider measures of (a) religiosity/spirituality (e.g., spiritual well-being scale), (b) functioning and faith (e.g., religious problem-solving styles), (c) God concept or one's emotional experience of God, (d) religious orientation (e.g., extrinsic religiosity), and (e) measures of one's personal experience of God (Hall et al., 1994).

Any number of these measures could be used to aid in the assessment of religious identity in a person's upbringing and family. The spiritual genogram, for instance, has been used by many therapists to obtain information about a family's religious and spiritual beliefs, values, and heritage (Hodge, 2001). Our focus should be on reaching a better understanding of the client's or the family's religious faith tradition, especially in relation to sex and gender norms, gender identity, and gender expression. We have found that even in cases where a young person navigating gender identity does not subscribe to their family's spiritual beliefs, that person's gender identity exploration could be impacted by messaging they received about gender while they were growing up.

Assessment of children. When we provide a consultation to a family with a young child, we assess the family's religious and spiritual background, as well as the extent to which their religious beliefs and values inform their response to their child's gender expression today.

When we meet with parents, we ask them whether religious or spiritual faith is a part of their current way of being in the world. As we noted above, a family's religious and spiritual identity is often why they are coming to see us rather than going to another specialty clinic, even when we have offered a referral to a larger, more comprehensive specialty clinic.

Because religion is often salient in the lives of the families we work with, we ask parents about the religious faith traditions they were raised in (broadly), as well as the local religious faith communities they have participated in (narrowly). We ask them how much of the faith they were raised in is a part of their life today, or how much it has informed the raising of their children, regardless of their current practices, using inquiries like the following:

- Tell me about your religious faith tradition growing up.

- How were your religious beliefs and values expressed in your home growing up?

- How much of the religious faith tradition you were raised in is a part of how you view things today?

We then move our assessment toward the questions these parents are raising about a loved one's gender identity. We ask how the faith they adhere to today addresses questions that arise around sex and gender.

- As you think about your religious faith tradition now, what have you found it teaches on sex and gender?

- How do teachings from your religious faith community inform your understanding of sex and gender?

- How do teachings from your religious faith community shape your response to your child?

Assessment of adolescents/adults. When we provide a consultation to a family with an adolescent—that is, any person between the ages of ten and nineteen—we assess the family's religious and spiritual background in much the same way we assess a family's background when they present to us with a young child.

When we assess an adolescent, however, we also ask the adolescent about the religious tradition they are being raised in (broadly) and their experience in their local community of faith (narrowly). That is, we want to have a better understanding of their experience in the Southern Baptist denomination, for instance, as well as what it has been like for them to be a part of Redeemer Church, for example.

As we do when we interview parents, we want to ask the adolescent how much of the faith tradition they were raised in informs their beliefs today. If they distance themselves from the family faith tradition or reject it outright, it may be helpful to understand what led them to that decision and whether that decision was related in any way to the tradition's teachings on sex and gender.

- Can you share a little about your religious faith community growing up?

- How much of the faith tradition you were raised in is a part of how you view things today?

- Can you share a little about what your religious faith community teaches about sex and gender?

- How have those teachings about sex and gender been communicated to you—either at your place of worship or at home?

- Which aspects of the teachings about sex and gender from your faith tradition are important to you today?

ASSESSMENT OF GENDER IDENTITY

Assessment of children. The field is not in agreement about the best way to evaluate children's gender identity, and we see a range of models being used at different specialty clinics. Berg and Edwards-Leeper (2018) provide a helpful overview of some of these different approaches. They highlight the general shift in the mainstream of the field away from assessment questions and measures that assume a pathology model and toward approaches that frame gender identities in terms of diversity. These now-prevailing approaches distinguish common gender exploration and gender-diverse experiences from gender dysphoria as it is currently understood in contemporary nosology.

Broadly speaking, this shift in the field is a move toward what is sometimes referred to as "gender affirmative assessment" (Berg & Edwards-Leeper, 2018, p. 103). Like previous assessment models, gender-affirmative assessment can include interviews with parents and the child, play therapy with the child, and psychological batteries that measure cognitive functioning or are otherwise intended to rule out possible co-occurring mental health or be-havioral issues. Regardless of which methods are used, gender-affirmative assessments seek to move away from traditional, normative assumptions about gender development and toward more open, child-centered ap-proaches that reflect an expanded vista for gender, gender expressiveness, and diverse gender identities.

When families approach us for a consultation, we inform them of other more comprehensive specialty clinics that are multidisciplinary and might offer a range of approaches to gender-identity assessment. However, many of our referrals desire to navigate gender-identity questions as individuals or families in ways that are sensitive to their religious beliefs. They have some-times chosen to come to our clinic after seeking services elsewhere and finding the assessment process to be hasty, feeling that their beliefs have been dismissed or undermined. A failure to assess religiosity, and how religion and spirituality interact with beliefs about gender, highlights again the impor-tance of cultural humility; clinicians must attend to religion and spirituality as important diversity variables among those we work with.

We describe our approach to gender-identity assessment as *balanced*, *client-centered*, and *without a fixed outcome*.[2] It is balanced because we locate ourselves between two more extreme positions: (a) those who are critical or dismissive of transgender and gender-diverse experiences and (b) those who, in an effort to be affirming of transgender and gender-diverse experiences, may do so without sufficient regard for contextual and other issues. We aspire to thoughtfully engage with the identified client and their family, recognizing that there are different lenses through which people see gender identity: in-tegrity, disability, and diversity. As we prepare for consultations, we try to locate different family members in terms of these lenses and begin to consider how these lenses shape expectations surrounding gender identity, gender role, and so on. We try to be mindful of how current cultural trends are under-stood by different stakeholders, including family members, their religious communities, and their other networks of social support and influence.

---

[2]As we mentioned in the preface, the phrase without a "fixed outcome" was part of conversations in a consensus panel from the American Psychological Association (APA) that provided input to the Substance Abuse and Mental Health Services Administration (SAMHSA) on appropriate responses to minors navigating sexual or gender identity.

We are also client-centered. We try to listen to our clients as they sort out their experiences of gender, both past and present; as they negotiate their beliefs about sex and gender; and as they determine how to move forward in their unique family and cultural context, taking into account their religious faith identity and how their faith informs their decision making.

We do not enter into therapy or into a consultation with a fixed outcome in mind. Our concern is not to push a priori conclusions about the best outcome of a client's gender-identity exploration, in keeping with the approach of others in our field (e.g., Sloan & Berke, 2018; Substance Abuse and Mental Health Services Administration [SAMHSA], 2015). We want to be open-ended, providing services without trying to force the experiences of our clients and families into a single mold. What our clients determine is best for them may range considerably from client to client as we consider a wide range of concerns.

One of the most important considerations we have found in assessment and subsequent care of a child is that parents focus on their unconditional love for their child as a starting point for their interactions around gender identity. When parents enter into the assessment process with assumptions about a normative or particular fixed outcome for their child, our experience has been that these assumptions can be experienced by their child as conditional acceptance. This is a tension we try to address early on. We do not know how a specific child will express their gender identity, how that expression will either stabilize or fluctuate over time, and what a child's gender identity will ultimately be; however, we do know that a child is best served by parents who express unconditional love and regard for their child.

We tend to rely heavily on parents in the assessment of children. However, it is important to make clinical observations of the child in addition to gathering parental reports. The goal of these observations is to gain a sense of how an outsider might perceive the child based on general impressions. You might think through such areas of gender presentation as clothing, hairstyle, and accessories (e.g., makeup, jewelry, purse, etc.), as well as voice inflection, gestures, and mannerisms. You can also ask yourself, How would someone who did not know this child perceive this child in terms of the child's gender and why? We typically also note the affect expressed by the child and any concerns they have about the consultation or counseling.

To supplement clinical observation of a child, we have found it helpful to obtain information from parents about what they see at home. This information can be collected over two to three weeks and involves a simple observational record of what parents see. We provide parents with a structure for identifying the kinds of behaviors and experiences that can help us determine whether a diagnosis of Gender Dysphoria is warranted (see worksheet 2.1). For example, we ask parents to make note of their child's gender-atypical play and activities, gender-related statements about themselves or themselves in comparison to others, preferences for clothing, and so on.

In one case, when preparing for a consultation with parents of a five-year-old child, we asked the parents to complete a daily parent observation form for a two-week period in advance of the consultation. The parents observed the child frequently pulling up his shirt in order to show his belly; selecting morning cartoons and stating, "I only want to watch girl shows"; asking to wear his mother's sweater; and going into his mother's closet and coming out with her heels on.

We also invite parents to share how they respond to gender-atypical behaviors in the moment so that we get a better sense for their concerns and their instincts as parents. These exchanges are significant to the counseling process because they can either contribute to a child's shame or convey a message of love. We have found that when parents experience significant anxiety in this area, they sometimes turn to fear-based parenting techniques they may later regret. A parent might respond to a boy wearing his mother's high-heeled shoes by sharply scolding him out of anger, for instance; it would be helpful for us to know about this pattern so that we can offer alternative responses.

Parents will often offer differing—and perhaps contradictory—records of what is occurring at home. For this reason, it may be helpful to have parents keep separate records. Clinicians should also get a sense for each parent's level of daily involvement with the child since factors such as a desire to please a same-sex parent or to hide gender-atypical play may influence parents' observations.

It may be helpful, too, to obtain information from a teacher about a child's behavior at school. This avenue of assessment must be weighed against whether the child's gender-identity exploration is something the family wishes for the school to be made aware of. Parents differ in their degree of comfort involving the school system at this stage of assessment—and as you can imagine, parents also disagree with one another about this from time to time. Some parents express concern that initiating this discussion with school personnel could be stigmatizing for their child, heighten the child's anxiety in social settings, or prematurely reveal something the child is still working to make sense of. In any case, if parents elect to ask a teacher to complete an observational form, this form covers similar kinds of experiences and observations: the child's gender-atypical play and activities, gender-related statements about themselves or themselves in comparison to others, preferences for clothing, and so on (see worksheet 2.2).

Interviews. Children are diagnosed with Gender Dysphoria only if six of the eight criteria listed below are met; the first criterion must be one of the six criteria that is met. These criteria must have been met for a minimum of six months. Children diagnosed with dysphoria also experience corresponding distress or impairment in social or educational functioning related to their gender identity.

The eight criteria are:

1. A strong desire to be of the other gender or an insistence that one is the other gender

2. A strong preference for wearing clothes typical of the opposite gender

3. A strong preference for cross-gender roles in make-believe play or fantasy play

4. A strong preference for the toys, games, or activities stereotypically used or engaged in by the other gender

5. A strong preference for playmates of the other gender

6. A strong rejection of toys, games, and activities typical of one's assigned gender

7. A strong dislike of one's sexual anatomy

8. A strong desire for the physical sex characteristics that match one's experienced gender (APA, 2013, p. 452)

Clinicians can proceed by asking about each of the eight criteria directly. For example, they can ask, When you consider the past six months, would you say that your loved one has a strong desire to be the other gender or insists that they are the other gender? However, we have found it much more helpful to interview around the topics in a more open-ended manner by asking parents to describe their child's clothing preferences, roles in play, preferences for toys, preferences for playmates, and so on. Here's what we mean:

1. When you consider the past six months, how would you describe the way your loved one has talked about or experienced their gender? [Probe for the parents' first awareness of their child's account of their gender, how the gender identity has been expressed over time, whether it fluctuates or is rather stable, and so on.]

2. When you consider the past six months, how would you describe your loved one's clothing preferences? [Probe for how much choice their child has in clothing selection, what kinds of clothing they would wear if it were entirely up to them, and so on.]

3. When you consider the past six months, how would you describe your loved one's make-believe play or fantasy play? [Probe for gender roles taken, whether these roles are assigned by an older sibling or peer, what roles the child prefers, and so on.]

4. When you consider the past six months, how would you describe your loved one's preferences for toys and games—what do they enjoy playing? What kinds of toys and games do they gravitate toward? What kinds of activities does your loved one enjoy? [Probe for the child's top two to three toys, top two to three games, and top two to three activities.]

5. When you consider the past six months, how would you describe your loved one's interest in toys, games, or activities that children of the same sex typically gravitate toward? [Probe by naming a few toys, games, and activities commonly associated with the same sex and listen for how the parents describe their child's response to those toys, games, and activities. Disinterest is not the same as strong rejection, but listen for how they describe their loved one's response to and experience with those toys, games, and activities.]

6. When you consider the past six months, who does your loved one most enjoy playing with—I'm thinking here in terms of their playmates? [Probe for preferences when they have options, and be sensitive to playmate availability in terms of who is in the home and neighborhood.]

7. When you consider the past six months, how would you say your loved one has responded to their own sexual anatomy? [Probe for any comments or questions about their sexual anatomy, a sense of identification with either parent by referencing sexual anatomy, and so on.]

8. When you consider the past six months, how has your loved one talked about or expressed interest in the physical sex characteristics of the other gender? [Probe for any comments or questions about physical sex characteristics, a sense of identification with either parent by referencing physical sex characteristics, and so on.]

We listen for whether the criteria of Gender Dysphoria are met as we go through our interview with parents. In order to help parents accurately gauge a six-month period during which symptoms could have presented, we might ask parents to think of an event that occurred at least six months ago, perhaps a birthday, a holiday, or some event that occurred in the news cycle. When they have chosen an event, we ask them to use that event to anchor their timeline so we get a more accurate picture of what the past six months have been like for their child. Answering questions regarding gender identity can be emotional for parents, making objectivity much more difficult at times.

In addition to conducting this kind of parental interview, clinicians can also utilize gender-identity-related parent measures. However, some of these measures have been normed on the previous *DSM* diagnosis (American Psychiatric Association, 2013) of gender-identity disorder (and may be in the process of being updated), and many have been evaluated as otherwise inadequate for a variety of reasons. We do utilize some parent measures with the understanding that there are inherent limitations to any measure today and that new measures are undoubtedly being developed for future assessment. Still, it is important to remain aware whenever possible of the latest and most widely accepted measures being used rather than relying on outdated measures.

Assessment of children with possible Gender Dysphoria should not rely on parent interviews and gender-identity-related parent measures alone.

Assessment can also entail the use of instruments for young children (under the age of six), instruments for children under the age of twelve, and additional instruments for parents and teachers (see Berg & Edwards-Leeper, 2018, p. 104). In some models of assessment, psychological testing protocols are recommended, and these include a measure of IQ, attachment, and personality, along with specific measures of gender identity (Berg & Edwards-Leeper, 2018, p. 105).

As we noted above, the field is not always in agreement about the best way to evaluate children, and there is a range of models being used at different specialty clinics. Some clinics do not offer comprehensive psychological testing, some perform initial screening and may recommend additional psychological testing, and still others focus primarily (and in some cases exclusively) on gender identity as such. In other words, some professionals today view these additional assessment instruments as unnecessary at the outset; that is, a clinician can do some basic interviewing or use standard semistructured interviews to determine if further evaluation of, say, cognitive development is warranted without feeling like such testing is necessary at the outset (Berg & Edwards-Leeper, 2018, pp. 105-6).

We also use the metaphor of a book with many chapters (see worksheet 2.3).[3] Parents can reflect on an older child's life and identify two or three chapters (or more) that they can title, and then they can identify key characters, themes, and so on, specifically associated with gender identity. We also invite parents to provide this information when we meet with adolescents.

Before we close this section on assessment of children, we should note that one of the more frequently cited concerns in the assessment of children is the potential for co-occurring autism spectrum disorder (ASD). Children who have ASD are diagnosed with Gender Dysphoria at a higher rate than children who do not meet criteria for ASD, and more information about the relationship between Gender Dysphoria and ASD is not well understood at this time. The current recommendations are for children to be assessed by a specialist in gender identity and a specialist in ASD (unless a specialist in both gender identity and ASD is available), and for the two specialists to work together on providing care to the child and family. In addition, it can be helpful

---

[3]A narrative approach has been used by McAdams and others to collect narrative data in support of theories of personality and identity; see McAdams (2001; 2014).

to utilize either ASD screeners or something like the Social Communication Questionnaire as a way of further assessing a child's social functioning and how this may or may not factor into Gender Dysphoria (Leef et al., 2019).

Assessment of adolescents/adults. As with our assessment of children, our approach to assessment of adolescents and adults is also to offer a *balanced, client-centered* gender-identity assessment *without a fixed outcome.* We obtain basic, preliminary information (see worksheets 2.4 and 2.5). We do not want to begin with an agenda in either direction with our clients. We try to remain balanced around a range of considerations that an adolescent or adult is weighing as they explore gender identity and any conflicts they may report between their gender identity and religious faith. We remain client affirmative and consider a range of options without a fixed outcome for gender identity.

The diagnosis of Gender Dysphoria is made with adolescents and adults only if two of the six criteria listed below are met. As with Gender Dysphoria in childhood, these criteria must have been met for a minimum of six months. There must also be corresponding distress or impairment in social or educational functioning. The six criteria are:

1. A marked incongruence between one's experienced/expressed gender and primary and/or secondary sex characteristics

2. A strong desire to be rid of one's primary and/or secondary sex characteristics

3. A strong desire for the primary and/or secondary sex characteristics of the other gender

4. A strong desire to be of the other gender

5. A strong desire to be treated as the other gender

6. A strong conviction that one has the typical feelings and reactions of the other gender (APA, 2013, p. 452)

The benefit to interviewing adolescent and adult clients is that you can now hear from them directly about their experiences rather than interviewing only parents and relying heavily on their observations about their child. When it is feasible to do so, we prefer to interview one or both parents as well as an adolescent client.

As in the case of parental interviews about their children, interviews conducted with adult or adolescent clients could include questions directly drawn from the criteria of Gender Dysphoria. For example, a clinician could ask directly: "In the past six months, have you experienced a marked incongruence between your experienced/expressed gender and primary and/or secondary sex characteristics?" (APA, 2013, p. 452). This would be the wording of the diagnostic manual, but it is not particularly accessible to most families we meet, and some adaptation would be helpful. Also, when we do ask direct questions, we again ask the adolescent or adult to think of an event or holiday that occurred at least six months ago. That event becomes an anchor in the timeline so we get a more accurate understanding of how the last six months have been for the adolescent or adult.

But rather than ask these direct questions, we tend to ask broader questions about gender identity. We have found it helpful to frame a client's experience of their gender identity as a book with many chapters. We then invite the teen or adult to title each chapter and share some of the key people in that chapter of their lives, the primary themes of that chapter, and so on. This approach helps us identify when the client's gender-identity experiences first came about (onset) and how their experience of gender identity has progressed over time (course), including how stable their gender identity has been and whether it has fluctuated.

For example, in our work with Layla, a twenty-one-year-old natal male who presented with a cross-gender identity, it was clear that Layla's gender identity had only been cross-gender for about three months. Layla reported that prior to that time her original experience of gender identity had been gender nonbinary (since shortly after puberty, around age thirteen). She denied any gender-atypical behavior or self-identification throughout childhood. In many ways this presentation would be considered an atypical case of Gender Dysphoria (late-onset). With such recent shifts in gender identity, it seemed more time would help everyone determine how stable Layla's cross-gender identity would be and what steps might be taken based on gender-identity stability or ongoing fluctuations.

When we work with adolescents, we have found it helpful to ask both parents and the adolescent to provide a narrative account of the adolescent's life; we then probe for the kinds of material that would help us determine if the criteria of Gender Dysphoria are met. We do the same when we assess adults.

As we discussed with the assessment of children, this narrative exercise can be done effectively using the metaphor of a book with many chapters (see worksheet 2.6). Clients might think of early childhood or childhood, from birth until age twelve, as the first chapter of their book. They might think of the next chapter as the beginning of adolescence. Some people divide their story into chapters that include elementary school, middle school, and high school.

Adults typically add a chapter on their early twenties or college age or age of vocational training. They might add a chapter or more beyond that as well, depending on their current age and other life experiences.

We also ask our clients to identify the chapter that led them to come into our clinic to speak to someone about their gender identity. This might be a different chapter from the chapter they hope to write during their time in counseling, which might be different still from the chapter they hope to write in the future.

For example, Finley, a fifteen-year-old natal female who identified as male, shared how the decision to come in for counseling felt like it was made by his parents. Although Finley assented to counseling, the chapter title he came up with for his current season was "What They Want." When we discussed with Finley what this title meant to him, he shared that he wrote it down as a reflection of what he felt his parents wanted for him—that is, to meet with a counselor to discuss his gender identity. We were careful to ask him what he wanted and whether counseling could be a part of that, especially if counseling could focus on specific goals he identified for himself or could improve his relationship with his parents.

Listening to and unpacking what chapter titles mean can help establish and strengthen the therapeutic alliance. It can also lead to discussions of goals for counseling that can be empowering for a client, because they might for the first time be asked what they want out of their time with a counselor. These discussions can lead to a new chapter, a chapter for counseling itself. The chapter might be titled "Clarity" or "New Direction" or "My Time"—some indication of the client's hopes and expectations for their time in counseling.

Another chapter you may want to discuss with clients is the next chapter they hope will be written once counseling has come to an end. Clients might speculate early in their counseling about what that chapter will be, but this is a topic worth returning to; clients often develop new ideas of what their next chapters might be titled on the other side of counseling, ideas that differ significantly from the next chapters they title as counseling is just getting underway. It is also possible to title a chapter/appendix related to questions or thoughts to explore in the future. This helps clients acknowledge that they will continue to sort out aspects of their experience and future steps even as therapy ends.

Outlining life by way of chapters can also help clinicians appreciate the range of messages a client may have received from key figures in their life—including parents, peers, youth ministers, pastors, mentors, siblings, and media—regarding gender identity and people who experience gender dysphoria. These insights are critical in identifying aspects of experience that may underlie the ebb and flow of overt gender-related distress.

For instance, Kit, a fourteen-year-old natal female who presented as androgynous, used she/her/hers pronouns for herself but also struggled with these pronouns. She reported a long history of gender-related distress and had not yet come to a coherent sense of gender identity when she came to see us with her parents. As early as age four, she would choose to play male roles in games; secretly dress in her older brother's clothing, including undergarments; beg her parents to let her cut her hair; and refuse to wear stereotypically feminine attire. Her parents, however, did not remember Kit's gender-related distress being as persistent as Kit described it. They recalled that, around middle school, she began to present as stereotypically feminine in dress and interests; she "was obsessed with makeup," and "her favorite color was pink."

When exploring the chapters of her life, Kit came to realize that she had heard messaging around this time from teachers and a pastor that "you need to stop acting like a boy," and her peers had been bullying her because of her presentation at school. Kit recalled her prayer life involving "asking God to take this pain away." She assumed that "if I act more like a girl, maybe I'll feel more like one too." Kit had never told her parents about these experiences until our consultation, which helped them appreciate the way her gender atypicality had fluctuated, even while her distress around gender had not shifted in the way her parents thought at the time.

Charting the timeline of a person's gender-identity journey can also help us identify the onset and course of any co-occurring concerns, including mood symptoms such as depression and anxiety, that may complicate gender-identity exploration or increase risk of self-harm. Some clients wonder if pursuing treatment for gender dysphoria will automatically alleviate co-occurring concerns. Clarifying the onset and course of these co-occurring concerns can clarify the degree to which these concerns coexist with or emerge from gender-related distress. Teasing these things apart—differentiating between dysphoria and depression, for instance—can help individuals and their families make informed decisions about courses of treatment, prioritize aspects of care, and set more realistic expectations for the alleviation of symptoms.

Exploring the onset, course, and timeline of gender-atypical behavior can also help clinicians distinguish early-onset dysphoria from late-onset dysphoria, as well as ruling out other possible diagnoses that must be considered before landing on a diagnosis of Gender Dysphoria. Some experiences that look at first like gender dysphoria may be motivated by another rationale. For example, a person might engage in gender-bending activities independent of their gender identity as a way to push back against cultural norms for sex and gender. We think of Jax, a fourteen-year-old natal male who identified as gay. He wore nail polish, shaved his legs, and dressed in female clothing periodically, which he reported was out of boredom. For him, these behaviors were not an expression of gender identity or a means of coping with dysphoria. He saw them as ways to challenge his parents' assertion of rigid gender stereotypes.

Fetish behaviors likewise do not in and of themselves reflect gender dysphoria, although gender dysphoria may develop later in concert with these behaviors. Consider the example of James, a natal male college student who sought treatment for what he described as "a strange addiction." Since the age of seven, James would periodically sneak into his sister's closet to wear her clothing and undergarments. At first, he simply felt curiosity; it was not until his mother found him dressed this way one afternoon that he felt immense shame about his experience. She never brought it up again, but he recalled in our work together that "her reaction said it all." "Good little boys never do stuff like that," she had said. So his shame began. He continued to engage in this behavior, taking care to keep it hidden.

When he hit puberty, James found himself aroused by this behavior, and it became even more laden with secrecy. James's faith was important to him, but as he grew older and began to feel more "disgusted" with his behavior, he came to believe that "God doesn't want to hear from me until I get this under control." In college, he learned from the media and peers about the reality of gender dysphoria. He resonated with these narratives, beginning for the first time to wish he was a female and feeling great conflict about the fact that he was not. In this case, James's gender dysphoria emerged from a fetish behavior; thus, our therapy with James dealt with both gender identity and with the original fetish.

Some teenagers seeking a sense of identity or community may find these things within the transgender community or broader LGBTQ+ community; others may turn to the language and categories we refer to as emerging gender identities (see Yarhouse & Sadusky, 2020). However, those who align themselves with transgender or emerging gender identities for such reasons may not meet criteria for Gender Dysphoria. We want to help these individuals understand their experience of gender identity without assuming Gender Dysphoria in every case.

We also ask adolescents and adults to rate their experience of incongruence along a scale. It is important to remember that gender dysphoria can reside along a continuum of intensity and can ebb and flow in a person's life. Dysphoria must be managed through day-to-day decisions, and some dysphoria can spike around particular events. The rating scale gives us a better sense for what clients are experiencing (see worksheet 2.7) and can lead to helpful discussions about their gender incongruence. We also ask them to rate their ability to cope with any dysphoria that may be associated with the incongruence. Coping strategies vary considerably and are often discovered through trial and error. This initial rating can lead to productive discussions about coping strategies throughout the course of therapy.

As with assessment of children, assessment of adolescents can vary considerably among specialty clinics. Some clinicians focus on comprehensive interviews of gender identity while others also include various gender-identity-related adolescent and parent measures. In some specialty-clinic models of assessment, psychological testing protocols are recommended: measures of IQ, attachment, and personality, along with specific measures of gender identity.

As we noted in our section on assessment of children, we tend to conduct a comprehensive gender-identity interview with the adolescent and the parent(s) separately, followed by gender-identity-related adolescent and parent measures and additional screening tools (for example, screening for depression) if the intake suggests that a co-occurring concern is likely present. Some clinicians would use fewer or none of these measures; others would add a complete psychological battery.

As we observe changes in the field today, we believe these different approaches reflect different assumptions about what is most helpful to an adolescent and their parents. What these approaches all tend to have in common is a desire to be as affirmational as possible in response to an adolescent who is exploring a gender-diverse presentation.

We noted early on in this chapter that it is important for clinicians to become aware of our own values and potential biases regarding a client's beliefs. It is also important for us to reflect on our beliefs and assumptions regarding gender, gender identity, gender expression, and gender roles. This self-reflection will help us assess gender-identity development and discuss a range of options with families of young children and adolescents, as well as discuss services with adults in a respectful and competent manner.

WORKSHEET 2.1. PARENT OBSERVATION FORM

Day:_____

PLAY	DESCRIPTION: MY RESPONSE:
MANNERISMS/ VOICE INFLECTION	DESCRIPTION: MY RESPONSE:
STATEMENTS	DESCRIPTION: MY RESPONSE:

My child's overall emotional state today:_____

_____

_____

My own overall emotional state today:_____

_____

_____

WORKSHEET 2.2. TEACHER OBSERVATION FORM

Day:_____

PLAY	DESCRIPTION: PEER RESPONSE:
MANNERISMS/ VOICE INFLECTION	DESCRIPTION: PEER RESPONSE:
STATEMENTS	DESCRIPTION: PEER RESPONSE:

Child's overall emotional state today:_____

_____

_____

_____

Child's overall relationships with peers today:_____

_____

_____

_____

WORKSHEET 2.3. NARRATIVE INTERVIEW WITH PARENTS

We tend to think of books as being divided into chapters. How many distinct chapters would you say you and your child have experienced together? For each chapter, please provide a title, the key theme associated with that chapter, and the key people. Write a brief account of what makes that time in your child's life a distinct chapter.

Chapter 1: _____

_____

_____

_____

Chapter 2: _____

_____

_____

_____

Chapter 3: _____

_____

_____

_____

Chapter 4: _____

_____

_____

_____

Chapter to bridge to counseling: When you think about the chapter of your life that led to the decision to come to counseling, how would you title that chapter, that decision? Again, who are the key characters, and what are the key themes associated with that chapter?

_____

_____

_____

Present chapter (counseling): If your life were a book with many chapters (some having been written, some you are writing now, and others you will write in the years to come), how would you title the chapter you are writing today? Who are the key characters, and what are the key themes associated with this chapter?

_____

_____

_____

_____

_____

_____

Future chapter: If your life were a book with many chapters (some having been written, some you are writing now, and others you will write in the years to come), how would you title the next chapter you hope to write? Who are the key characters, and what are the key themes associated with this chapter?

_____

_____

_____

_____

_____

_____

What are the questions/thoughts that linger for you that you may want to delve into in the future? How will you continue to explore these thoughts/questions?

_____

_____

_____

_____

_____

_____

Note to clinician: In each chapter, in addition to title/theme/people, listen for how the parents describe what counts as masculine or feminine behavior in a child and how frequently those behaviors are present in their loved one.

WORKSHEET 2.4. ADOLESCENTS: PRELIMINARY INFORMATION

Experienced gender (check one): _____boy _____girl _____transgender _____nonbinary _____prefer to self-describe: _____

Anatomical sex (check one): ____male ____female ____intersex

Pronouns (check one): ____ he/him/his ____ she/her/hers ____ they/them/theirs ____ Other: _____

I have dressed exclusively as a _____ for _____ (months/years)

I have sometimes dressed as a _____ for _____ (months/years)

If you have made changes in dress related to gender identity, when did you first make these changes? _____

How were you referred here? _____
_____

Have you been evaluated by another mental health professional or gender program?
_____Yes _____ No

If yes, please list the mental health professional or gender program, indicating the dates of treatment and the reason you discontinued: _____
_____
_____
_____

PERSONAL HISTORY

Please briefly describe what you think your concerns are:

_____

You are here for professional services. How will you measure whether the professional services were helpful to you?

_____

DESCRIPTION OF SELF

How do you describe yourself today?

_____
_____
_____

WORKSHEET 2.5. ADULTS: PRELIMINARY INFORMATION

Experienced gender (check one): _____man _____woman _____transgender
_____nonbinary _____prefer to self-describe: _____

Anatomical sex (check one): ____male ____female ___intersex

Pronouns (check one): ____ he/him/his ____ she/her/hers ____ they/them/theirs ____ Other: _____

I have dressed exclusively as a _____ for_____ (months/years)

I have sometimes dressed as a _____ for_____ (months/years)

If you have made changes in dress related to gender identity, when did you first make these changes? _____

How were you referred here? _____

_____

Have you been evaluated by another mental health professional or gender program?

_____Yes _____ No

If yes, please list the mental health professional or gender program, indicating the dates of treatment and the reason you discontinued: _____

_____

_____

_____

PERSONAL HISTORY

Please briefly describe what you think your concerns are:

_____

You are here for professional services. How will you measure whether the professional services were helpful to you?

_____

DESCRIPTION OF SELF

How do you describe yourself today?

_____

_____

_____

WORKSHEET 2.6. NARRATIVE INTERVIEW WITH ADOLESCENT/ADULT

We tend to think of books as being divided into chapters. How many distinct chapters would you say you have experienced with respect to your gender? For each chapter, please provide a title, the key theme associated with that chapter, and the key people. Write a brief account of what makes that time in your life a distinct chapter. Be sure to offer some description that covers elementary school years, middle school years, and high school years among the various chapters you choose to describe.

Chapter 1: _____

_____

_____

_____

Chapter 2: _____

_____

_____

_____

Chapter 3: _____

_____

_____

_____

Chapter 4: _____

_____

_____

_____

Additional chapters (as needed):

_____

_____

_____

Chapter to bridge to counseling: When you think about the chapter of your life that led to the decision to come to counseling, how would you title that chapter, that decision? Again, who are the key characters, and what are the key themes associated with that chapter?

_____

_____

_____

_____

Present chapter (counseling): If your life were a book with many chapters (some having been written, some you are writing now, and others you will write in the years to come), how would you title the chapter you are writing today? Who are the key characters, and what are the key themes associated with this chapter?

_____

_____

_____

_____

Future chapter: If your life were a book with many chapters (some having been written, some you are writing now, and others you will write in the years to come), how would you title the next chapter you hope to write? Who are the key characters, and what are the key themes associated with this chapter?

_____

_____

_____

_____

What are the questions/thoughts that linger for you that you may want to delve into in the future? How will you continue to explore these thoughts/questions?

_____

_____

_____

_____

Note to clinician: In each chapter, in addition to title/theme/people, listen for how the client experiences their gender identity, whether it appears to be rather stable or somewhat variable, and so on.

WORKSHEET 2.7. INCONGRUENCE AND COPING

Directions: People experience different degrees of incongruence between their gender assumed at birth and their gender identity today. People also live with different tolerances for the incongruence they feel. Some people are able to live with a high level of internal gender dysphoria. Some people are *not* able to live with this high level of incongruence.

1. Make a mark on the first line below (which shows a continuum from very low to very high) that shows your current experience of gender incongruence.

   My experience of gender incongruence:

   _____

   very low   low   moderate   high   very high

2. Then make a mark on the second line below that shows your current ability to cope with your experience of gender incongruence.

   My current ability to cope with gender incongruence:

   _____

   very low   low   moderate   high   very high

(Reproduced with permission from Yarhouse, 2015)

Look at your marks on the two continuums above and reflect on these questions:

1. What does your rating of your sense of incongruence mean to you?

   _____

   _____

   _____

   _____

2. What does your rating of your ability to live with gender incongruence mean to you? What are some of your current coping strategies?

   _____

   _____

   _____

   _____

3

DISCUSSING THE GENDER
AND RELIGIOUS IDENTITY
THERAPY APPROACH
WITH CLIENTS

THIS CHAPTER WILL EXPLAIN how to discuss the client-centered, Gender and Religious Identity Therapy (GRIT) approach with clients and to determine whether a client is a good fit for this approach.[1] You will also learn how to obtain advanced informed consent from clients, whether you are working with adult clients or with the parents of children and adolescents.

In chapter one we discussed three lenses through which people view diverse gender-identity experiences (including gender dysphoria, transgender experiences, and emerging gender identities). Yarhouse (2015) has described these three lenses as *integrity*, *disability*, and *diversity*.

When we think of providing a consultation or ongoing therapy to a person or family navigating gender identity and faith, we recognize how people view gender-identity experiences through these different lenses. We recognize that the integrity lens's assumptions about sex and gender resonate with many conventionally religious people. At the same time, we recognize that some experiences of gender identity seem to challenge the integrity lens, and many

---

[1]The reader may be aware, too, of the concept of grit as developed by Angela Duckworth (2016), which has to do with "passion and perseverance for long-term goals" (Angela Duckworth, FAQ, https://angeladuckworth.com/qa/#faq-125). Grit is often understood in relation to academic achievements and professional success (along with IQ, talent, humility, social intelligence, etc.). People can cultivate grit by fostering interests, practice or habits, sense of purpose, and hope. While using the acronym GRIT, we are not drawing on the same conceptual framework, although we do see among those we work with a kind of perseverance and meaning making that is reminiscent of the concept of grit with quite different applications.

religious people—especially young people—may find themselves drawn to the disability or diversity lens.

These three lenses inform how we think about our professional services to those navigating gender-identity concerns. When we meet with clients and their families, we listen for the lenses each person may rely on in their understanding of gender dysphoria, transgender experiences, and emerging gender identities. We try to help each person identify their own lenses and the lenses of others who have a stake in the decisions being made. This process can be particularly useful if one of your goals is to help a person navigate gender-identity and religious-identity conflicts or to improve family relationships. We encourage each family member to consider why different people are drawn to different lenses, increasing their capacity to empathize or to see through the eyes of the other. When family members disagree, the lenses can help them understand why they disagree, especially when someone has previously struggled to articulate principles they care deeply about. By emphasizing mutual understanding and common goals, family members will be better equipped to express their love for each other even in the midst of contentious conversations around emotionally fraught and personally relevant topics such as gender identity.

We try to offer more than just empathy and perspective, however. We provide consultative and ongoing therapy services in light of an *integrated lens* that draws on the best of these three lenses. While an integrated lens might look different for different clinicians, we tend to think about our integrated approach this way:

1. We recognize ways in which sex differences are meaningful to and inform the lives and values of many people with whom we have met (integrity/sacred lens).

2. We respond compassionately to those managing gender dysphoria and to those navigating conflicts around gender identity and religious identity, appreciating the distinct challenges that emerge when gender identity and personal faith create tension intrapersonally and interpersonally (disability/departure lens).

3. We create a clinical setting in which clients are able to explore personally meaningful questions of identity and community, honor their

own uniqueness, and ultimately uncover a path forward toward thriving (diversity lens).

We share this basic understanding of the three lenses and our integrated approach in our advanced informed consent form (see worksheet 3.1). We explore with our client the questions they have about this approach, how it differs from other available approaches, and to where they can turn for alternative options if this approach is not a good fit for them. We also discuss past therapy experiences and any ways in which they feel hesitant to integrate faith/spirituality in their work. This is important given the range of clinical approaches many of our clients have encountered and their appropriate mistrust of providers who may have devalued an aspect of their experience or taken an approach to therapy around gender identity that has caused harm.

When co-determining goodness of fit, we want to understand the relevant aspects of diversity that will be important to explore and integrate over the course of a person's work in therapy. We explain that, for some people, spiritual/religious identity will inform and be interwoven with their gender-identity exploration, and they are seeking an approach that accounts for that. For others, while spirituality or gender identity, or both aspects of identity, are important diversity variables, the actual exploration of gender identity is not relevant to their therapeutic goals. The latter is a case where we would discuss the importance of honoring these variables but would not move into a GRIT approach in our work. The principles underlying this approach may very well be relevant, but the actual interventions would not draw from the GRIT model.

When working with individuals and their families, we also want to discuss the importance of adequately assessing for co-occurring concerns that may complicate a person's process of navigating gender identity. We have found that not everyone who comes into therapy will understand and take seriously the importance of treating anxiety, depression, and other mood symptoms. Many families we have worked with have come to therapy to prioritize supporting a loved one navigating gender identity. We have found that some people can feel confused when therapy involves discussing topics beyond gender. One example would be in the case of family members witnessing the deep pain of a loved one's gender dysphoria and appropriately feeling a sense of urgency to assist their loved one in this regard. We have met with family members who want so badly to "take away the pain" of their loved one that it can feel irrelevant to talk about anything other than the best steps to take regarding gender identity. In these cases, family members can fail to see how much family dynamics may actually heighten the barriers to the exploration process. In shifting the focus to the identified client, the family may not come to terms with the importance of using therapy, especially family therapy, for different family members to take responsibility for or address the dynamics that preclude a person from adequately exploring gender identity. When this happens, and in anticipation of the possibility of it, we want to name the tensions individuals and families will feel within this work and the need for open communication about familial factors that will likely need to be understood and addressed along the way. We also want to normalize the reality that no journey is done in isolation. By naming this, we can also highlight the important role of family in this process insofar as their involvement is desired by the client.

As we mentioned earlier, we always share with clients that other professionals could provide more comprehensive, multidisciplinary services in the area of gender identity. We offer referrals to those sites whenever clients desire them, especially if they wish to obtain a second opinion when considering specific steps forward. We want to provide as many adequate resources as possible to individuals navigating this space. We want clients to have the freedom to say that our approach is not a good fit for them and to consider other pathways that better suit their needs.

Having discussed how we talk about clinical services with our clients and reviewed the content of advanced informed consent, we now want to briefly discuss several practical issues that arise when providing services to transgender persons and those navigating questions of gender identity and faith, as well as their families. Attending to these issues will better equip you to offer quality and ethical care within a balanced gender-identity approach.

PRACTICAL ISSUES

Use of names/pronouns.

Aubrey and her parents came in for an initial consultation. Aubrey was a fourteen-year-old natal male who identified as female and introduced herself with the name Aubrey and female pronouns. As we sat down, Aubrey's father said matter-of-factly, "I should get one thing out of the way up front: We are not comfortable with the use of the name Aubrey. We named our child Lucas, which has special meaning for my wife, and we are just not able to use the name Aubrey right now."

Aubrey stood up: "Wait, what? I know this has been a bit of a shock, but Aubrey is how I am known at school and by my friends. I've been asking for this for months now. You are the only two people who don't respect what I've asked for. I'm not coming in here every week to hear my deadname. No way."

One practical issue to think about is how you will respond to different requests for the use of names and pronouns, particularly when working with couples or families. We nearly always use the name and pronouns our clients use to identify themselves. We understand this to be a gesture of clinical hospitality and appreciation for the journey that the person before us is on, as well as a means of entering into this person's journey at its current chapter. When have there been exceptions? Sometimes when we work with adolescents, for example, there can be sharp disagreements between parents and teens over whether to use the name and pronouns with which the teen identifies, as in the case of Aubrey. We usually stop the session at that moment and ask the parents to enter into a conversation with their child about how to move forward in counseling, highlighting the bind this puts us in clinically. In other words, we could use the name/pronouns the parents ask us to use, but this will likely leave us unable to form a therapeutic alliance with the teenager, who could view us as aligning with their parents and prone to say or do anything their parents tell us to say or do. Alternatively, if we use the name/pronouns the teenager asks us to use, but do so without the parents' support, we may connect with the teen, but we will likely see the teen pulled from therapy services by the parents.

How do we proceed in such difficult interactions? We ask the parents and the teen to talk about and reach a decision about language in our work together, and we document the verbal agreement of family members. When we invite the family to make this decision together, it affords us the opportunity to observe how the parents and teenager communicate with one another. It also affords us the opportunity to observe the family's capacity for problem solving and perspective taking. We have seen several resolutions that move the care forward. Sometimes the parents say, "Ultimately, we just want our child to talk to someone. It may not be where we are with all of this, but if it's important and will help our child open up to someone, so be it." Other times the teen defers to their parent's wishes: "Look, I know I only broke this news two months ago, and my parents are really struggling to catch up. It's okay for now, and maybe we can revisit names and pronouns after a little while." Still other times, the family comes up with a nickname, maybe a name the teen was referred to as a younger child (such as Star) that has no gendered elements creating difficulty for either the parents or the teen.

When it comes to documentation, many documentation platforms have a location for legal name as well as a location for preferred name or nickname. When this is possible, we would write the legal name and the name used by the client in the appropriate sections. We have also found it helpful, insofar as the name used by the client changes over the course of therapy, to document in a progress note that this change has occurred. This is especially true if pronouns used by the client have shifted. We would want to record why pronouns used in documentation have changed, and a statement in a note is important to address this. We often will state that, "per client's request, and with verbal approval of the parents, notes will utilize [he/him/his; she/her/hers; they/them/theirs] pronouns from this point forward."

Importantly, we have found that some people feel hesitant to assert their desire for their chosen name and pronouns. This is especially true when others have been unwilling or unable to honor their name/pronouns or when individuals are worried about being a burden. Consider the story of Clare.

> *Clare presented to therapy and shared that they have been wrestling with gender-identity questions for the last two years. When asked about their pronouns, Clare said, "I don't really care. You can use she or they. People use both."*

We felt it was important to ask Clare whether their ambivalence was motivated by genuine indifference about which pronouns we used or if it was rooted in a desire to not inconvenience us. When we discussed this distinction with Clare, they realized they had come to feel like a burden to others, and this feeling informed their reluctance to ask for the pronouns that resonated with their current experience of gender identity.

It is also important to discuss the use of name/pronouns in the medical record. In our records, we note both a client's legal name and the name/pronouns with which they identify. We also discuss with clients (and their families, when relevant) how we plan to document our sessions and take notes during consultations. Insofar as you are working in a group practice, or alongside multiple providers who care for the same client, it is important to ensure that all of the staff are on the same page regarding documentation. This is especially important because clients may ask to gain access to their records or be transferred to another mental health provider at some point. Various staff members (some of whom may not have a background in psychology) often need to be educated about the rationale behind what name/pronouns your practice uses for certain clients. This is where training of staff becomes an essential part of laying a foundation for the therapeutic work you will do.

Training staff.

Emery is a sixty-two-year-old natal male who in the course of therapy began hormone therapy and presents as a woman. Emery's voice, however, is rather deep and does not reflect her gender identity. When Emery called the clinic one day to cancel and reschedule an appointment, the new receptionist referred to Emery with male pronouns. Emery was hurt, expressing frustration and even anger toward the receptionist. Our next session began with a discussion about how injurious the exchange with the receptionist was to Emery.

We have learned the importance of training support staff to use the names and pronouns with which our clients identify. Administrative staff often have phone contact with clients but do not have the same visual reference points or sustained relationship a therapist might have with a client who has adopted a cross-gender or other gender identity. A staff member may simply respond to the sound of a person's voice, which may or may not be a reliable indicator of the speaker's gender identity.

It is important to allow clients like Emery to process experiences in treatment where they have been hurt by the careless words or actions of staff, as when staff mistakenly referred to Emery by different pronouns than those she uses for herself. Such ruptures afford the opportunity to explore other moments when Emery has been impacted by actions that evoked similar emotions. By processing these emotions, Emery can consciously determine how she would like to respond to such difficulties if they arise in the future.

As we mentioned previously, it is important to educate staff about the value of using the names and pronouns of clients, anticipating the salience of both positive and negative exchanges to clients, and practice responding in moments when gender identity may be unclear.

Restrooms. For therapists seeking to offer balanced therapy to gender-diverse people and those exploring gender identity, another important consideration is the availability of restrooms for individuals seeking treatment. Many clinicians use shared workspaces, and these spaces do not always have options available for clients like Emery who might feel uncomfortable or unsafe using the restroom that matches their gender identity. Clients may prefer to use a single-stall restroom or a family restroom if one is available and easily accessible. If none is available, some clients have chosen to use the bathroom that matches their gender identity; others have refrained due to safety concerns, especially in certain regions of the country, and may instead use the bathroom that matches their birth sex. Still others have chosen to refrain from using clinic restrooms altogether due to discomfort or difficulty determining which option would feel safest for them.

It is essential that your clients know the options available to them, discussing early and often in therapy how they would like to make decisions about bathroom use. Especially insofar as a person's gender identity shifts over the course of therapy, they will need to consider bathroom options and decide how to weigh these options; they may even wish to make this decision process a focus of therapy.

WORKSHEET 3.1. ADVANCED INFORMED CONSENT

NAVIGATING GENDER AND RELIGIOUS IDENTITY

This is a consent form for therapy exploring gender identity and religious identity. This form is available to you because you are requesting therapeutic services with respect to your gender identity and religious identity. Please read and sign it to indicate that you understand and agree to participate in our approach to therapy.

The way we address care is through a client-centered, gender and religious identity therapy (GRIT) approach, which allows clients to explore gender and religious faith and any conflicts between these two aspects of identity. This therapy emphasizes the exploration of gender identity without a fixed outcome, the attainment of coping skills, and the establishment of social support.

Informed consent is an important part of our work together. It helps us establish treatment goals with clients in a collaborative manner. This form will provide background information as part of informed consent.

When we refer to gender identity, we are referring to a person's psychological experience of themselves as a man or woman (boy or girl) or another gender identity (such as genderfluid or gender nonbinary).

Identify what is causing concern. In our experience, people come to see us for one of several possible reasons: (a) to clarify a diagnosis of Gender Dysphoria (if present), (b) to receive a diagnosis and/or treatment recommendations for any co-occurring concerns (e.g., depression), (c) to discuss treatment recommendations specific to gender identity and religious identity, and (d) to improve family relationships that may have been strained in the context of gender-identity questions or concerns.

Lenses through which people see gender. We believe there are at least three lenses through which people frequently look at gender dysphoria: *integrity*, *disability*, and *diversity*. The *integrity* (or *sacred*) lens is based on widely held traditional understandings of male/female differences that reflect sex and gender norms. The lens perceives certain inherent differences between how males and females ought to behave, what one theologian refers to as an "essential maleness" and an "essential femaleness."[2] To violate these categories of essence is, according to the integrity lens, to violate the ethics of gender.

---

[2]The theological underpinnings of this lens are discussed in Yarhouse (2015), *Understanding Gender Dysphoria*, pp. 46-48.

In contrast to the integrity lens, the *disability* (or *departure*) lens sees gender incongruence as a predictable variation that occurs from time to time (or, in this case, quite rarely). It is not an ethical infraction, simply a departure from the norm. Within this lens, gender incongruence and associated gender dysphoria might be understood as unfortunate nonmoral realities to be addressed with compassion.

The third lens is the *diversity* lens. This is the lens toward which broader Western culture is rapidly moving, and it is the one most frequently represented in the medical and mental health professions. The diversity lens views gender incongruence not as a concern to be corrected (integrity) or as a condition to sympathize with (disability) but as a difference in experience that reflects a different kind of person. That is, there are cisgender kinds of people and transgender kinds of people, and the experience of being transgender should be celebrated as an expression of diversity. Some of the most vocal advocates of the diversity lens call for the deconstruction of sex and gender norms because these norms are sometimes considered oppressive.

These three lenses inform how we think about our professional services to those navigating gender-identity concerns. When we meet with clients and their families, we listen for the lenses each person may rely on in their understanding of gender dysphoria, transgender experiences, and emerging gender identities. We try to help each person identify their own lenses and the lenses of others who have a stake in the decisions being made. This process can be particularly useful when a goal is to navigate gender-identity and religious-identity conflicts, or to improve family relationships. We encourage each family member to consider why different people are drawn to different lenses, increasing their capacity to empathize or to see through the eyes of the other. When family members disagree, the lenses can help them understand why they disagree, especially when someone has previously struggled to articulate principles they care deeply about.

But we try to offer more than just empathy and perspective to our clients. We provide consultative services in light of an *integrated* lens that draws on the best of all three lenses. Concisely put, our integrated lens looks like this:

1. Recognize ways in which the integrity of sex differences may be meaningful (integrity/sacred).

2. Respond compassionately to those managing gender dysphoria (disability/departure).

3. Explore questions of identity and community that are meaningful for all people (diversity).

We shared in our initial communication with you that there are other competent professionals who provide more comprehensive, multidisciplinary services in this area. We would be glad to provide you again with the names and contact information for those specialty clinics.

During our consultations, we will try to collect information that helps us make an accurate diagnosis of Gender Dysphoria and co-occurring concerns (such as depressive disorders and anxiety disorders). We almost always recommend treating co-occurring concerns first; we do not want a person making weighty decisions about gender dysphoria out of a state of significant depression, for example. Exceptions to this idea of treating co-occurring concerns first would involve times where a thorough evaluation suggests the experience of gender dysphoria is significantly contributing to depression/anxiety or the level of distress associated with gender dysphoria is life threatening.

We have found it helpful to think of various treatment options for gender dysphoria as *management strategies residing along a continuum*. Before people come to see us, they have often already taken initial steps to manage their gender dysphoria through trial and error. We will work with you to locate your own existing strategies along that same continuum and to identify what has been helpful or unhelpful to you.

In most cases of gender dysphoria occurring in late adolescence or adulthood, the dysphoria is unlikely to resolve on its own. We are not aware of any research-backed approaches to therapy that help clients resolve their gender dysphoria in keeping with their birth sex. Much of the field has focused on helping people cope with their gender dysphoria, often supporting cross-gender identification to assist with coping.

Clinical services to minors are particularly controversial. We can discuss with you various approaches clinicians sometimes take when working with minors, including current trends in care. The approach we follow is that of gender-identity exploration without a fixed outcome. This is the language used in a Substance Abuse and Mental Health Services report on care for sexual and gender minority youth.

It is also possible to delay puberty medically through the use of puberty blockers, gaining more time to make a decision about what steps to take later. We can discuss options like this one—and the anticipated benefits and the controversies surrounding them—in the context of our consultation.

When working with older adolescents and adults, the frame of reference we use is this: *What might it look like to manage gender dysphoria in the least invasive way possible?* This language reflects the integrated lens we mentioned. It is least invasive for many reasons: it includes elements from the integrity lens; it reflects an openness to intervention in light of the disability lens; and it keeps fundamental needs for identity and community in view out of regard for elements of the diversity lens.

To understand what we mean by least invasive, think of intervention or management strategies as residing along a continuum. They can range from quite minor (e.g., changes in hairstyle or clothing) to much more substantive (e.g., surgeries). There are many management strategies that reside between the poles of this continuum; most people do not elect the most invasive strategies. The World Professional Association for Transgender Health (WPATH) describes the steps along this continuum as *reversible, partially reversible,* and *irreversible.* These categories can be another helpful way to organize various interventions.

The approach we take to gender identity is informed by the idea of milestones: specific events and experiences identified as important by adults who experience gender dysphoria. The list of milestone events and experiences from which we draw has been developed through research among transgender Christians and other transgender persons of faith, especially those navigating gender-identity and religious-identity conflicts. Milestones for such individuals include events both related to gender identity and those informing faith identity.[3] Of course, these categories often overlap since people tend to make meaning out of their experiences in light of their personal or religious beliefs and values.

---

[3]See M. A. Yarhouse and T. L. Carr (2012), MTF transgender Christians' experiences: A qualitative study. *Journal of LGBT Issues in Counseling, 6*(1), 18-33; T. L. Carr, M. A. Yarhouse, and R. L. Thomas (2014), Report on TG Christians' milestone events, in B. L. Miller (Ed.), *Gender identity: Disorders, developmental perspectives and social implications,* Nova Science, 281-83; and T. L. Carr and M. A. Yarhouse (2014), God and the transgender person, in B. L. Miller (Ed.), *Gender identity: Disorders, developmental perspectives and social implications,* Nova Science, 271-79.

The prominent role that gender dysphoria now plays in larger cultural debates about sex and gender can make it difficult to know how best to respond to your own concerns about your gender identity or that of a loved one. We encourage you as much as possible to set aside these broader debates in order to focus on what our field of study "knows" and does not know about gender dysphoria. Once you have reflected on the three lenses of integrity, disability, and diversity, we encourage you to reflect on the range of management strategies available to you so you can make an informed decision about how best to proceed.

Services provided to minors. Generally speaking, minors must obtain permission from a parent or guardian to receive most mental health services, including a consultation regarding gender identity. If parents are bringing a minor in for a consultation or ongoing therapy, we ask that the minor indicate if they assent to professional services by signing the informed consent form.

Services provided to couples. Recommendations can also be offered to couples in which one person is navigating gender-identity concerns. For these couples, we generally follow the same model we use when working with couples negotiating sexual-identity concerns.[4] We may recommend that both the partner navigating gender-identity concerns and the other partner receive parallel individual services before seeking out joint couples counseling.

Consent to therapy. I have read this document, have had an opportunity to discuss its content with my provider, and have agreed to its terms. This authorization constitutes informed consent to the GRIT approach to gender identity in consultation or therapy. A photocopy or facsimile of this form and signature(s) shall be considered as valid as the original.

Client Signature _____ **Birth date** _____ **Date** _____

Parent(s) Signature(s) _____ **Date** _____

Clinician's Signature _____

---

[4]M. A. Yarhouse & J. L. Kays (2010), The PARE model: A framework for counseling mixed orientation couples. *Journal of Psychology and Christianity, 29*(1), 77-81.

PART 2

THERAPY POSTURES AND GESTURES— CHILDREN

4

GENDER PATIENCE

IN THIS CHAPTER WE INVITE YOU to consider an appropriate clinical posture toward children and their families. Our goal is to adopt a flexible posture in our clinical work, allowing us to respond to the experiences and needs of each child and their family. The posture we take is important because it gives us clinical flexibility in an important and contested area of mental health service delivery.

There have historically been three basic approaches (or postures) to therapeutic services to children with gender dysphoria (Yarhouse, 2015; Zucker, 2020a). These approaches are (a) facilitating resolution with the child's birth sex, (b) watchful waiting, and (c) facilitating resolution with the child's experienced gender identity.

The first approach, facilitating resolution with the child's birth sex, is not practiced frequently today to our knowledge. Several states have identified such practices as gender-identity-change efforts (GICE), akin to sexual-orientation-change efforts (SOCE), and have legislated against these practices. We mentioned some of these developments in the preface.

Some professionals (e.g., Cantor, 2018) have pointed out that all the research conducted to date has been on SOCE, not GICE, and that equating one with the other is problematic on both conceptual and empirical grounds (Cantor, 2018). However, absent such research, we can say little about the effectiveness or existence of any therapeutic protocols or interventions that resolve gender identity with a person's birth sex. What we do know from the stories of gender minorities is that, as they reflect on past experiences of therapy where the goal was conformity to one's birth sex, there are reports of interventions that were not helpful, and in some cases harmful, ultimately not accomplishing that goal.

The second approach, watchful waiting, takes a wait-and-see posture to the gender identity of a prepubescent child. Proponents of this approach cite empirical evidence suggesting that most children who experience gender dysphoria do not continue to experience their dysphoria into late adolescence or adulthood.

It is difficult to anticipate the future of watchful waiting as an approach to care. The American Academy of Pediatrics (AAP) recently criticized watchful waiting as "outdated" in a policy statement:

> This outdated approach does not serve the child because critical support is withheld. Watchful waiting is based on binary notions of gender in which gender diversity and fluidity is pathologized; in watchful waiting, it is also assumed that notions of gender identity become fixed at a certain age. (Rafferty et al., 2018)

The AAP policy statement has been criticized on several grounds (e.g., Cantor, 2018), including the lack of research on practices referred to in the statement as "conversion therapy" and the statement's failure to account for studies in which children's gender dysphoria was reported to have desisted in adolescence or later.

The third approach, facilitating resolution with the child's experienced gender identity, means aiding in a child's gender transition or in the consolidation of a child's social gender transition through reversible changes such as name and pronouns, clothing, and hairstyle. This approach has sometimes been criticized when it involves medical interventions. As we noted in the preface, some states have created bills aimed at curbing any medical interventions for minors (with the precise age of restriction varying based on the bill under consideration).

The differences between these three approaches represent differences in professional thought, philosophical assumptions, and "deep structure variations in theoretical perspectives on the nature and nurture of psychosexual differentiation" (Zucker, 2020a). We believe the vast majority of mental health professionals are well intentioned and want to protect children who experience gender incongruence or gender dysphoria, or who otherwise reflect diverse gender identities. However, sometimes the desire to serve a marginalized group can get ahead of the empirical research in a specific area of concern. Likewise, well-intended counsel may be rooted in beliefs and values not shared by everyone with a stake in the conversation and can do harm to a person navigating gender identity. Just as we have discussed (and will continue to discuss) fear-based ways of parenting, there can be fear-based ways of doing research, providing clinical services, and establishing policy statements out of these approaches. Mental health professionals and other parties involved must seek to identify and address the underlying fears that can drive these endeavors so as to reduce the ways that fear-based approaches create undue challenges and obstacles for individuals and families seeking support. This is why we advocate for a client-centered approach, recognizing that offering a fixed outcome for each person negates the multiplicity of resolutions possible for people who seek care around gender.

A related area of professional disagreement has to do with how to conceptualize children who meet criteria for gender dysphoria in childhood but do not meet criteria in adulthood. How ought these children to be understood differently from those who meet criteria for gender dysphoria both in childhood and in adulthood? This question is sometimes called the "persister/desister debate."

THE PERSISTER/DESISTER DEBATE

Some professionals distinguish between two groups of children with gender dysphoria, *persisters* and *desisters*. *Persisters* are those whose Gender Dysphoria, initially diagnosed in childhood, persists into adolescence and adulthood. *Desisters* are those whose Gender Dysphoria, initially diagnosed in childhood, desists as they go through puberty or shortly thereafter. Proponents of this distinction cite studies (e.g., Steensma et al., 2011) that report relatively high rates of desistance and attempt to identify differences among persisters and desisters (see figure 4.1). (It should be noted that while desistance of gender dysphoria was reported in these studies, there appears to be an increased possibility of a nonheterosexual identity as a long-term outcome, which will raise the question of parental capacity to be supportive of that possibility as well.) According to some reports, such as Steensma et al. (2011), persisters tended to believe that they were the other sex, had a negative response to puberty, and were less receptive to gender-typical interests. Meanwhile, desisters wished they were the other sex (but knew they were not), feared puberty but experienced it as a consolidation of their gender identity, and were ultimately receptive to gender-typical interests (for a review of existing research, see Cantor, 2018).

PERSISTERS' EXPERIENCES

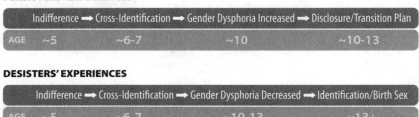

(Steensma et al., 2011)

Figure 4.1. Contrasting desister/persister trajectories (Steensma et al., 2011)

Other professionals assert that there are no persisters or desisters but that the data reflect categorical differences among types of children. For example, Ehrensaft (2018, p. 42) describes these children as "apples" and "oranges." In this typology, apples are children who could be classified as persisters: "They demonstrate cross-gender identifications early in life and continue with these identifications into and beyond puberty" (p. 43). In contrast, oranges are children sometimes called desisters. These children "are gender expansive in their gender presentations but do not repudiate the sex assigned to them at birth, finding it a fine fit as long as they are not policed in their gender expressions" (p. 46). Ehrensaft later added "fruit salads" to the typology to account for children who were different from both apples and oranges. These children are "gender weavers who make a tapestry of self, which is neither male nor female but their own creative understanding of gender, both in identities and expressions" (p. 48).

While Ehrensaft's nomenclature makes it easy to identify apples and oranges once children have gone through puberty and reached the other side of their gender-identity exploration, it remains remarkably challenging to know with confidence during a child's initial exploration which category they will fit into in the long term. This uncertainty makes decisions about specific interventions, such as puberty blockers and hormone therapy, very difficult for families. We will discuss these decisions in subsequent chapters.

In our previous work (Yarhouse & Sadusky, 2020), we express concern that professionals may not fully appreciate the field's participation in what

Ian Hacking (1995) describes as a "looping effect." That is, the way in which professionals counsel children contributes to the development of new categories and linguistic constructs for understanding, experiencing, and enacting emerging gender identities. Rather than "the children leading us," as Ehrensaft has suggested, mental health professionals and others may contribute to the creation and expansion of seemingly endless gender expanses in front of children and adolescents, who adopt our new language and categories and reflect them back to us. The professionals who determine what counts as "knowledge" in the realm of gender do so by hearing their clients speak using categories they have given to these clients. Thus, attempts by professionals to study and respond to emerging gender identities contribute to the further deconstruction of sex and gender norms.

Our experience is that many specialists in gender identity would not be particularly concerned with the observation we are making. That is, even if they were to concede that recent developments have in some way eroded norms around sex and gender, many specialists would support such an erosion. They often view the sex/gender binary as a source of oppression to transgender and gender-diverse persons. This may be the case; however, it does not negate the concern that the erosion of norms may exacerbate the very kinds of experience that make these norms come to seem oppressive. Also, shifts in norms create space for new language and categories that contribute to people coming into existence in terms of how they think about themselves and their identity, expression, and history (Yarhouse & Sadusky, 2020, p. 32).

Counseling, of course, is where we attempt to locate family members in these discussions and experiences of changing norms and language. Where beliefs and values can become a conflict is in work with conventionally religious families in which their own beliefs and values support the binary and are a part of their faith tradition in a meaningful way. We cannot state enough that clinicians need to consider how they will navigate these conversations, especially across differences in beliefs or values, in service of the mental health and well-being of a child in their care.

A flexible clinical posture: scaffolding, gender patience, and exploration. We are not as confident as some of our colleagues in clinicians' current ability to predict desistance and persistence. We also recognize that some professionals in this area would frame this less as a matter of prediction than as a more general acceptance that gender identity may be constantly evolving and different aspects of transition (for example, social or medical) may be part of an exploration process, such that decisions to change course away from transition do not reflect a mistake as such.[1] Perhaps research in the areas of persistence and desistance will take great strides forward in the coming years, but at present the research offers little guidance for this challenging clinical task. We recognize that for children who do eventually transition, a wait-and-see approach may seem like delaying the inevitable. However, until we have reliable measures of persistence and desistance (if these distinctions continue to be meaningful), we worry that we cannot accurately predict which patients will be helped by an earlier transition and which may suffer additional harm. We also urge professionals to try to understand sex and gender through the eyes of parents for whom these decisions are layered with additional complexities vis-à-vis religious beliefs and values.

In the GRIT approach (figure 4.2), when we meet with families of younger children, we develop the analogy of a scaffold. A scaffold is a temporary structure placed around an object, such as a building, so that the building can be built or restored (see figure 4.3). Once the work is complete, the scaffold is removed and the building can stand on its own. In our analogy, scaffolding refers to a temporary parental framework that is available and supportive as gender identity develops.

The scaffold we advise parents to create around gender identity is not meant to manipulate a child's gender-identity outcome.[2] Remember that we

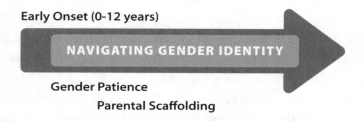

Early Onset (0-12 years)

NAVIGATING GENDER IDENTITY

Gender Patience
Parental Scaffolding

Figure 4.2. Gender and religious identity: younger children

[1] Thank you to Dr. Diane Chen for offering her perspective on this aspect of the persistence/desistance discussion.

[2] We do not introduce this analogy as an educational tool for learning new concepts à la Vygotsky; rather, we introduce it as a parental posture, an image to help parents and guardians locate themselves in relation to their child and their child's unfolding gender identity.

are focusing on the *exploration* of gender identity without a fixed outcome in children who appear to experience a conflict in their gender identity.[3] The scaffold, then, is a parental frame or structure that provides safety and security for a child to explore gender identity while the parents exercise gender patience.

The scaffolding parents provide to children navigating gender-identity questions must be sensitive to both the parents' beliefs and the child's need for emotional and spiritual safety. We want parents to place a premium on creating emotional and spiritual safety for their children. Creating safety involves not overreacting to gender-atypical interests, mannerisms, voice inflection, activities, or questions. This can be difficult for some parents. We find that parents often have fears about raising a child whose gender atypicality seems sustained. These fears can range from

Figure 4.3. Parental scaffolding

having a child who is transgender, to raising a child who will be mistreated in a world that does not respond well to gender atypicality, to whether they or their loved one will incur divine wrath due to their gender identity and behavior. When these fears are not worked through, parents may respond to their child in a fear-based manner, saying or doing things they would not ordinarily say or do. We do not want parents to parent out of fear because of their own anxieties, doing relational damage to their child in the process.

---

[3]We are not suggesting scaffolding without a fixed outcome for children whose gender identity appears well established, as it does for the vast majority of children.

For this reason, parental scaffolding will be most emotionally and spiritually safe when parents are able to name their fears and work through those fears in therapy, perhaps alongside other parents who have navigated similar terrain. Doing this work with parents strengthens their capacity to scaffold without allowing their fears to wound their child. Since many parents are highly focused on their child and the child's needs at this time, it is important to help parents reflect on what they—the parents—might need at this time. As parents practice scaffolding, they may need to process their own responses to their child's exploration, and collateral sessions are incredibly helpful toward this end.

Scaffolding can also involve generous supportive comments, expressions of unconditional love and acceptance, teachable moments, appropriate limit setting or redirection, and safety planning for interactions with the child's peer group. Scaffolding takes place in the broader context of gender patience as parents are encouraged not to get ahead of gender-identity development and expression.

Gender patience means refraining from foreclosing prematurely on gender identity when a child expresses gender-atypical interests or behaviors. In the GRIT approach, parents who adopt a posture of gender patience allow their child to explore which forms of behavior and self-expression feel most authentic to them. During this time of exercising gender patience, clinicians can support parents in a number of ways. Mental health providers can

- provide psychoeducation on the current professional discussions and controversies surrounding "persisters/desisters" and "apples/oranges."

- offer to explore gender identity with a child in the context of play therapy.

- seek referrals for parents to process their own reactions and challenges related to parenting a child navigating this space.

- connect parents with supportive group environments where they could learn from other parents who are on (or have recently been on) similar journeys with a child.

- help parents learn assertiveness for challenging unhelpful or shaming responses from loved ones, members of their faith community, and so on related to a child's gender atypicality.

- help the child connect to sources of passion to channel their interests and talents in a way that offers community, identity, and a sense of mastery of an aspect of their life, even while gender identity may be a point of tension.

- help siblings foster close relationships with the child, bolstering support for the child and reducing tension in the home.

- offer a range of coping skills to navigate experiences like depression, panic, and anxiety that may complicate a child's exploration and inhibit self-esteem.

Gender patience is a flexible posture that allows for a wide range of gestures from parents. Being supportive, providing encouragement, redirecting, educating, and safety planning are all potentially important gestures. In contrast, rigid postures will limit gestures, and we want to expand the options of gestures for people to take. We call this posture gender patience because we encourage parents to patiently observe the gender of the child without reacting purely in fear. Indeed, the reactions that many children interpret as parental impatience are often fear-based. Transgender adults tend to report that parental reactions that emerged from fear were among the most harmful to them during their own youth.

Not all approaches to therapy encourage gender patience and open-ended exploration of gender identity. Approaches that insist on integrating a child's gender identity with their natal sex or on promoting transition, although they target opposite goals, share an expectation that only one outcome should be pursued. Both approaches seek to overlay a fixed outcome onto every child, an outcome often based on assumptions (whether spoken or unspoken) about the nature of gender identity and the child's best interests. Consider this example:

Nate and Vicki are parents in their late thirties who come for a consultation with a seven-year-old natal male. They recall that as far back as two years ago Logan asked to wear a dress outside as part of a game with his sisters. In the last eight months or so, Logan has talked about wanting to be a girl. Two months ago, Logan put on a dress and tights and said to his mother, "I wish God had made me a girl." Most of Logan's gender-atypical behavior has to do with clothing and hair. Logan will sometimes put a towel around his head and declare to his mother, "I've got long hair like you have long hair."

What do scaffolding, gender patience, and identity exploration look like for this family? While they could take many forms, here are a few ways this family chose to adopt a posture of gender patience. When Logan picked out a doll for himself from a box of hand-me-downs and began sleeping with it in his bed each night, his parents did not raise any objections. They did make a rule that Logan's doll must stay at home when they are out running errands; however, they made the same rule for their daughter, who is a year younger and would also like to bring her doll along on errands. Logan's parents did not shame him for his interest in dolls, but they did identify consistent ways to set boundaries with all of their children.

A new family recently moved into Nate and Vicki's neighborhood. That new family had a little boy about Logan's age. Logan had been playing with his sister and her girlfriends for an hour or so. Vicki told Logan about the family, particularly the little boy, and asked, "Do you want to go meet him?" Logan said, "No." Again, this was fine with Nate and Vicki. There was no need for them to force male friendships onto Logan or to limit his play time with girls. These actions would likely be experienced as shaming by Logan, who might begin to wonder what his parents thought of him and what was wrong with his current preferences. Vicki and Nate could continue to create opportunities for male friendships as they presented themselves without overreacting to Logan's preferences or forcing him into relationships or activities he elected not to pursue.

There are dozens and dozens of daily moments when parents might try to manipulate events in a way that allays their fears. Such manipulation may set a parent's mind at ease, but it is not helpful to a child who is gender atypical or is otherwise exploring questions about gender identity. Parents are most helpful when they are nonreactive, emotionally even-keeled, warm, and supportive of their child. They may need at times to redirect their child or set limits on specific behaviors, but such moments should not be emotionally charged and should not leave a child feeling shamed or embarrassed.

For Logan, playing with his sister and her friends served as a kind of safe haven, providing him with a secure relational milieu. He was accepted for his interests and able to explore his preferences without being teased or bullied. Nate and Vicki planned to talk to Logan in the future about how some of his friends may not want to play in the same way as his sister and her friends;

they may not understand his interest in wearing a dress or sleeping with a doll. Parenting for Nate and Vicki involved prudence about how to reduce Logan's risk of teasing or peer-group rejection. This prudence meant that Nate and Vicki might clean up certain toys during some of Logan's afternoon playdates. But Logan benefited from having safe areas to play and to develop and express his interests in the company of others.

Each developmental stage brings a new set of challenges. Parents will want to recognize the challenges of each stage and the fears associated with these challenges. Recognizing and naming their fears helps parents begin to work through these fears, which can reduce their reliance on fear-based parenting tactics.

Cultivating family relationships. Given the current sociocultural climate around gender identity, many people highlight the importance of children's autonomy, with or without the ongoing support of their families of origin. Some urge movement away from maintaining familial bonds, especially if parents or other family members are struggling to understand a child's gender-identity conflict. We can appreciate this shift, given the ways we and others have seen harm done to children by family rejection. However, the quality of the parent-child relationship is the most significant predictor of the child's well-being over time (Katz-Wise et al., 2016). Thus, it is important to maintain parental relationships and improve their quality wherever possible (see Yarhouse & Zaporozhets, in press). Of course in the cases of abuse and neglect related to a child's gender identity, or in otherwise unsafe home environments, family relationships may need to be severed in order to prioritize safety. In general, however, we encourage therapists to assert the value of family relationships in a child's life.

In order to strengthen these relationships, we have found it helpful to connect parents to support resources. In particular, we have seen great value in linking Christian parents to others navigating similar family challenges. Whether this connection comes through formal group-therapy environments or through informal support groups and online forums, parents have gained a great deal from realizing they are not alone. It has been said that when young people "come out of the closet" as LGBTQ+, their parents "go in the closet." When parents are isolated and under strain, having no safe places to explore their own reactions to their child's gender identity, their wrestling can manifest in unhelpful ways, even in shaming their child.

Educating others. When families choose to approach gender identity with patience, one challenge they often face is the way others interpret and respond to their approach. We have seen some pastors, ministers, and other support people presume that parents' patience and scaffolding signify apathy about their child's decisions. Others assume that anything other than pursuing a cross-gender identity is rejecting and damaging. An already complicated parental experience is made even more difficult when so many voices weigh in without adequately understanding the gender-patience approach.

Take, for instance, Ken and Joyce, Christian parents who came to us for a consultation. They were wrestling with how to care for their ten-year-old, Casey, who was periodically found borrowing her older brother's undergarments and became tearful any time she was expected to wear dresses or skirts. One night her parents overheard her praying, "I wish I was a guy. God, please make me a guy." When Ken and Joyce shared this experience with fellow Christians at their church, they received two broad responses. One was to urge them to intervene by "course correcting" Casey toward femininity: "Take her to get her nails done, have Joyce spend more time with her one on one doing things that help her see it's not so bad being a girl, and find her more female mentors." The other response was to tell Ken and Joyce that Casey must begin identifying as male: "Let her do whatever she wants. She knows herself best—who are you to get in the way of self-discovery?" Ken and Joyce, though, didn't want to push their daughter one way or the other. They had heard that course correction can be shaming and painful for those whose gender-identity concerns persist but also that for many children like Casey, gender-identity concerns may desist at puberty.

In talking with Ken and Joyce, we shared how they could journey alongside Casey without a fixed outcome. More importantly, we offered to explain the gender-patience approach to important leaders in their life who would be supporting them through this discernment process. They were relieved to find that they did not need to justify every aspect of their approach with others; we could be a resource for people in their lives, specifically pastors, who might want to understand the approach.

For some people navigating gender identity, gender patience leads to important moments of decision making. We turn now to consider one of the many significant decisions clients may make about gender identity and ways to position yourself as a mental health professional during the decision-making process.

5

APPROACHING PUBERTY

Answering Questions Around Puberty Blockers

Easton, age eight, was brought in by his parents, Lisa and Jim, for a gender-identity consultation. Easton was a natal male who had been displaying gender-atypical mannerisms and interests since the family had moved from out of state to their new home five years ago. Lisa and Jim initially thought of any gender atypicality as likely a response to the upheaval of moving, a "phase" that would pass if they gave it time, or possibly within the "normal limits" of what other boys might do. But as time went on, both parents expressed concern that there could be real gender-identity "confusion," as Lisa put it. Once Easton was formally diagnosed with Gender Dysphoria, his parents raised the question of whether to consider puberty blockers. Lisa and Jim still hoped Easton's dysphoria might resolve on its own, but they wanted to at least begin a conversation about the decisions they might face in the years ahead if the dysphoria continued.

Sandor is a twelve-year-old natal female who came for a gender-identity consultation with his parents. Sandor has presented as a boy for the past eighteen months and made a full-time social transition about six months ago. Sandor struggles with anxiety, which has been increasing in intensity in recent months because of his fears about going through puberty. Sandor's parents do not report any gender-atypical experiences in Sandor's childhood, although Sandor remembers some events differently. This makes it especially difficult to determine the onset or course of the dysphoria. However, all parties agree that Sandor today experiences gender dysphoria and is in considerable distress. They are preparing to meet with a pediatric endocrinologist and wish to have an evaluation of gender identity prior to that meeting.

This chapter addresses the question of whether to use hormone blockers with children just entering puberty. If Easton's gender dysphoria worsens or does not abate in a few years, is blocking puberty something Lisa and Jim should consider? What about Sandor? Puberty is imminent, and his anxiety is through the roof. How should his parents respond?

Let's first discuss what puberty blocking is. In 2007, pediatric endocrinologist Norman Spack introduced hormone blockers in the United States as an intervention for youth diagnosed with Gender Dysphoria (Boghani, 2015). Hormone blockers had already been used in the Netherlands for many years under the Dutch model of care for gender-identity concerns. Puberty blockers themselves were originally developed for the treatment of precocious puberty.

Although many gender specialists do not consider puberty blocking to be a medical intervention in the same way the use of hormone therapy is a medical intervention, blocking puberty does involve changing a child's body chemistry through the use of gonadotropin-releasing hormone analogs (hormone blockers). The intervention itself was not originally intended for its current use. Spack recommends that blockers be given at the early stage of puberty—what is referred to as the Tanner 2 stage of development (Ruttimann, 2013). This keeps the gonads from producing either testosterone or estrogen, thus delaying puberty by preventing a natal female from beginning her menstrual cycle or developing breasts or preventing a natal male from growing facial or body hair or experiencing a deepening of his voice.

Those who argue in favor of using puberty blockers observe that their use was originally intended to buy time. Also, if a child eventually adopts a cross-gender identity, their physical transition will be much easier if they never develop secondary sex characteristics corresponding to their birth sex. For example, if Easton were to go through puberty as a boy, he would have a more difficult time later presenting as female because of his height, his bone structure, and the development of an Adam's apple, among other changes in puberty.

Those who are critical of puberty blocking point out that a high percentage of older children experience a lessening of gender dysphoria by late adolescence or early adulthood. These critics might elect to have a child experience puberty to see whether puberty helps to consolidate a child's gender identity in ways that reflect the child's birth sex. Critics also observe that there is relatively little research on puberty blocking, and what has been published raises concerns about its impact on bone density and cognitive development (Ruttimann, 2013). It is also unclear whether puberty blocking accomplishes its stated purpose of buying time before more permanent conclusions about a child's gender identity can be reached. To date, studies suggest that children who undergo puberty suppression are far less likely to adopt the gender identity corresponding with their birth sex. That is, rather than creating space for a child "to decide *either* to adopt the gender identity corresponding with their birth sex *or* to adopt a cross-gender or other gender identity, blocking puberty seems to weight the decision, making children far more likely to ultimately choose a transgender or alternative gender identity" (Yarhouse & Sadusky, 2020, p. 54). It is unclear, however, that the number of children who utilize blockers and eventually medically transition do so because of the blockers themselves or because of the onset and course of gender dysphoria in those studies. In other words, the early studies from the Netherlands were of children with early-onset gender dysphoria (no late-onset cases) who also underwent comprehensive evaluations prior to medical interventions. (See fig. 5.1.)

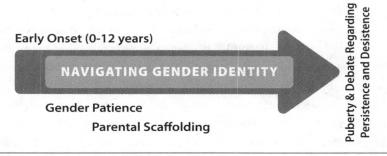

Figure 5.1. Locating the decision about puberty blocking

As we turn to the roles of the counselor and gender specialist, it will be important for professionals in both roles to emphasize that blocking is not the first step in a series of steps that lead to an inevitable outcome but that blocking is intended to "push pause" and allow for further exploration of gender identity.[1]

The counselor. If you are a mental health professional working with children like Easton and parents like Lisa and Jim, you may be wondering about your role in this decision-making process. Here are a few things we would want a clinician to do. First, we recommend that counselors seek additional training opportunities to understand the experiences of those

---

[1]Thank you to Dr. Laura Edwards-Leeper for her thoughts on the use of puberty blockers.

exploring gender identity and current trends in care. Results from a task force survey published in 2009 by the American Psychological Association found that only 30% of practicing and training psychologists report feeling familiar with gender dysphoria or diverse gender experiences (APA, Task Force on Gender Identity and Gender Variance, 2009). Well-meaning clinicians can do harm when they lack training and experience. Balanced education and training are an essential starting point to ensure ethical care when individuals face important decisions such as these.

Second, keep in mind that a multidisciplinary team is likely involved in this decision-making process. This team could include a mental health professional, a primary care physician, a gender specialist, and a pediatric endocrinologist or other medical provider (Hendricks & Testa, 2012). There may also be one or more representatives of the family's faith community, such as a pastor or children's minister. One of the most helpful things a clinician can do is facilitate communication among these different providers.

A counselor could focus on building and supporting Easton's self-esteem (Edwards-Leeper et al., 2016). Children's sense of their value and worth as a stable reality is a key part of resilience, increasing their capacity to navigate some of the storms they may face as they negotiate their gender identity. If Easton can see himself as increasingly able to develop his personality, gifts, and talents, he will be better equipped to root his sense of self in aspects of his identity that may feel more stable at a time when his gender identity does not.

Counseling can also be a place to develop coping skills, especially tactics for managing difficult peer or social interactions. Although Easton is only eight years old, we would want him to be equipped with a range of coping strategies if he were to have a difficult social interaction at school or in his neighborhood. The risk of these adverse social experiences is part of what makes Easton's home environment, and especially his relationship with his parents, important to attend to. The potential negative impacts of difficult peer interactions will be buffered if Easton's home environment is a safe haven for him to make sense of these experiences without internalizing unhelpful messaging. As noted in a key resource for adult transgender care, "in the absence of learned adaptive coping strategies, a complex clinical picture can emerge" (Sloan & Berke, 2018).[2]

---

[2] See the other articles in Kauth and Shipherd (2018) for more information regarding coping and appropriate interventions with adults.

Counseling can also be a safe environment to provide support in cases of teasing or bullying. Coping skills can help Easton in the moment a difficult peer interaction occurs, but he will also benefit from having a safe environment (in addition to home) supporting him if he experiences teasing or bullying. Therapy can supply that safe environment. Once safety has been established in therapy, we try to foster greater safety in the home and other significant environments like church and school. Easton could learn how to identify and challenge unkind comments as well as identify people he can turn to for support in navigating these comments when they arise.

Finally, a counselor can offer ongoing assessment of and intervention around any mental health concerns. Children sometimes internalize their stress through stomachaches or externalize their stress through disruptive behavior in school or at home. We want to help alleviate stress when we are able. In addition, we want to monitor cases where stress may result in disruptive behavior or be somaticized and lead to physical complaints. We must also be vigilant for perhaps unrelated but still co-occurring concerns that may develop, including symptoms of depression or anxiety.

The gender specialist. The gender specialist is a valuable addition to Easton's care team. If a diagnosis of Gender Dysphoria is warranted, the specialist would be the most appropriate person to make or confirm this diagnosis. They could also differentiate co-occurring concerns and make recommendations for addressing these concerns. Insofar as the specialist forms an ongoing relationship with Easton, they could be a support for Easton's exploration of gender identity. In our model of care, this exploration would be open-ended, without a fixed outcome.

A gender specialist could also meet with Lisa and Jim to provide education on decisions they may eventually face, such as whether to consider puberty suppression. The specialist can help parents understand what goes into this decision, what questions they could ask their medical provider, and so on. In addition, a specialist could prepare Lisa and Jim to make the most of every other appointment in the weeks and months ahead. They could discuss what happens to a child's body at puberty if there is no intervention to suppress puberty, as well as what happens with suppression (Chen et al., 2018; Edwards-Leeper et al., 2016). Finally, they could make recommendations for ongoing counseling with the individual/family therapist involved in Easton's care. They could collaborate with school counselors as well in navigating the impacts of a social transition or puberty blocking on a child's experience of school and peer relationships.

The religious leader or ministry coordinator. A supportive religious leader or ministry coordinator can be a valuable source of support for a family within their faith community. If misunderstanding or gossip arises about what the family is navigating, this faith leader could provide encouragement to the family while educating others in their community about the decisions the family is facing. This person could also help a family decide how much of their journey they want to disclose to others in their faith community and when that disclosure should happen.

A pastor could use their authority within their faith community to emphasize the importance of loving Easton for who he is and the qualities he possesses, regardless of unknowns moving forward. They could discourage gossip among other ministry leaders, emphasize that someone else's story is not theirs to share, and remind leaders to get permission from the family to share with other staff or church members. They could bring in experts to train staff on gender identity. They could also develop connections with Easton's counselor in order to gain insight on how to respond to bullying or other negative reactions Easton might face within their faith community. They could also identify mentors to offer one-on-one support for Easton, insofar as certain ministry programs are not yet equipped to offer what is needed to foster his personal spirituality.

A children's ministry coordinator could support Easton by taking care not to shame or pressure Easton to conform to rigid gender stereotypes, and by helping others in their ministry do the same. They could be a sounding board for any parents in their ministry who may have questions about Easton. Of course, they should first discuss with Easton's parents how to navigate such questions and conversations while honoring the privacy of Easton and his family. Depending on the kind of relationship this ministry coordinator has with Easton, they could offer to be a listening ear as Easton wrestles with how his personal faith and friendships might be impacted by his gender-identity exploration. If this kind of support would not be fitting based on their relationship with Easton, they could at least offer another set of eyes on Easton to observe how he functions in different settings, making note of any emerging challenges that could be helpful for parents or a mental health professional to be aware of.

Just as parents often need to identify and confront their fears about having a child or teen navigating gender identity, religious leaders and ministry co-ordinators may also need to identify and confront fears of their own as they provide support to families navigating gender identity and religious identity. Recognizing and working through these fears can help religious leaders avoid fear-based ministry tactics that could have unintended consequences for a child or teen and their family.[3]

A WORD FOR PARENTS AND OTHER SUPPORTS: AVOID REJECTING BEHAVIORS

Research on children navigating diverse gender identities (as well as on ado-lescents navigating sexual identity) has distinguished between "accepting" and "rejecting" parental behaviors. In your role as a clinician, offering this list to parents, family members, ministry leaders, clergy, and teachers who con-sult with you can be especially helpful as a starting point for conversation around helping and not harming. Conventionally religious individuals may not be able in good conscience to engage in all the behaviors classified as "accepting" since some of these behaviors may conflict with parents' convic-tions about sex and gender. However, it is essential for parents and other supports to identify and eliminate the following "rejecting" behaviors:[a]

1. Causing physical injury (hitting, slapping) to a child who has gender-identity questions.
2. Name-calling or otherwise doing verbal injury to a child navigating gender identity.
3. Not allowing a child to participate in family activities because they have gender-identity questions.
4. Blaming a child if they are harassed or bullied for being gender atypical.
5. Putting pressure on a child to be more masculine or feminine.
6. Suggesting that God will punish a child for having questions about their gender identity.
7. Suggesting that you are ashamed of the child for having questions about their gender identity.
8. Keeping a child's gender-identity questions a secret from others (against their will) so that they are unable to talk about their questions.

---

[3]For additional recommendations for ministry, see Yarhouse and Sadusky (2020), esp. chaps. 4-9.

There are good empirical reasons for urging parents and others to avoid these kinds of rejecting behaviors. Such behaviors have been associated with increased risk of suicide attempts, depression, use of illegal drugs, and engagement in unprotected sex. Eliminating such behaviors is a good and important place to begin, and counseling can be a next step in learning how to positively accompany a child navigating gender-identity questions.

[a]Adapted from C. Renna (2009), *Family rejection of lesbian, gay and bisexual adolescents & negative health outcomes*, Family Acceptance Project, San Francisco State University, https://familyproject.sfsu.edu/news-announce/family-rejection-lesbian-gay-and-bisexual-adolescents-negative-health-outcomes.

A multidisciplinary approach. One of the mistakes we have seen among clinicians supporting children like Easton is that they seek to do so independent of other supports. That is, mental health professionals too often seek to support children like Easton without collaborating with his parents and family, ministers, mentors, gender specialists, endocrinologists, and so on. Conversely, we have noticed that members of faith communities are often not equipped to engage in conversations about gender identity without the insights of mental health professionals. This is especially true in communities where therapy, mental health, and gender-identity exploration are stigmatized. In light of this dynamic, one of the most strategic things a clinician can do is attend to the distinctive dynamics of the faith community.

We have already mentioned that one role of the mental health counselor may be to educate faith leaders, and that both faith leaders and counselors may benefit from education by gender specialists and endocrinologists. We also want to emphasize that faith leaders, members of a faith community, and family members themselves are integral in helping mental health professionals and medical providers understand the beliefs and values that may influence a family's decisions as they navigate gender-identity questions. In other words, education can move in all directions. This is especially true if a medical or mental health provider does not come from the same religious background as a family or has little experience navigating the values of a particular belief system.

Ultimately, Easton and his parents did decide to meet with a pediatric endocrinologist. The parents came to a collateral therapy session first to talk through their questions and concerns so that they felt more prepared for this meeting. Upon meeting with the endocrinologist, they decided that, given several concerns they had and the recognition that Easton was currently experiencing some relief from dysphoria through the use of other adaptive coping skills such as changes in hairstyle and dress, they would not move forward with the use of blockers at that time. They talked about how helpful it was to get their questions answered and know what they were saying "no" to, and know where to turn if the dysphoria worsened in such a way that blockers would be a consideration again.

Cultural humility. We want to close with a reflection on the value of cultural humility in addressing the difficult decisions families face (Sadusky & Yarhouse, 2020). To steamroll over deeply held religious convictions, or to discount medical and mental health perspectives as a matter of principle, is to fail to adequately address the real challenges families face. If as clinicians we do not offer a posture of cultural humility to the families we work with, they will come to fear mental health professionals and deem us incompetent to support them on their journey. Failure to exhibit cultural humility has had catastrophic consequences in the past; some families have chosen not to seek out any mental health support for their child because they fear their beliefs will be pathologized or outright negated.

Regardless of your own lens for viewing gender identity, cultural humility is a demanding task. Even a very nuanced lens that integrates gender identity with other aspects of diversity, including religion and spirituality, must still leave room to hear and learn from those who think differently. Cultural humility invites clinicians to model teachability, curiosity, and a capacity to hold tension among multiple stakeholders. These principles can provide a guiding light for clinicians as we seek to support families, many of whom will have a range of sometimes contradictory perspectives.

As many therapists already know, our role is often to model behaviors and interactions family members and other sources of support can emulate. When parents see a therapist model teachability, curiosity, and a capacity to hold difficult questions in tension, this good example will likely be far more effective than if the therapist simply told them how they ought to parent. When we tell parents how to parent, they often push back immediately and resist change. We find that clinicians are better served when we demonstrate strategies of engagement that allow all family members, parents and children alike, to maintain their convictions while still acknowledging they have a lot to learn. This demands more creativity on our part to consider how to reflect strategies of relating that can be enacted by a range of different people.

Mental health professionals cannot model a culturally humble posture if we do not continue to explore and seek consultation on the ways our own beliefs, values, and experiences inform the work we do with our clients. The same is true when engaging with other specialists and pastors or ministry coordinators. If clinicians seek merely to correct others rather than listen to them, we will often lose the trust of those we are speaking to, thereby alienating a range of people necessary to the success of each child.

PART 3

THERAPY TOOLS— ADOLESCENTS AND ADULTS

6

ADOLESCENCE

A Brief Overview

Audrey and Allen shared that when their daughter, Kate, age sixteen, said she had something she needed to tell them, they thought that she was going to say she was gay. They had their suspicions because Kate wasn't all that interested in dating. But when Kate shared that she was transgender, they were "stunned." They hardly knew what to say.

Mateo came with his parents for a consultation on gender identity. He is fourteen and says he is gender nonbinary. His parents express concern for him, and they don't know what to make of the idea of a "nonbinary" gender. They had wondered about their son from time to time because he was not particularly interested in the play and activities that other boys pursued. But they figured it would all work itself out eventually.

Olivia, age seventeen, came with her mother for a gender-identity consultation. She and her mother agreed that she had long had a reputation for being a "tomboy," something that was true for Olivia's mother when she was growing up. But for Olivia it was more than that. She reported feeling confused by her gender at a young age, as young as four or five. She believed she was a boy, but she didn't know how to put it into words. "It was just all very confusing to me," she shared.

Cho is a sixteen-year-old teenager who came to a consultation with her parents. Cho has recently shared that she is trans, which has led to multiple difficult discussions in their home. The parents are asking for help because Cho has asked them to use male pronouns. The parents say that they feel shocked and that they cannot talk to anyone about this, confident that no one in their family would understand.

As we approach gender-identity exploration in adolescence, it can be helpful to understand whether the adolescent is experiencing gender dysphoria that is a continuation of gender dysphoria from childhood, which is early-onset, or whether the adolescent is experiencing gender identity concerns for the first time, which is late-onset. Clinicians should obtain this information from their assessment to help guide the understanding of the gender-identity journey of the young person they meet with. It can be helpful to understand onset and course because there is currently more research on early-onset cases that extend through to adolescence and adulthood while there is less research available on late-onset cases and how best to support those navigating these experiences.

We will discuss specific therapy tools for working with adolescents and adults in subsequent chapters, but we offer in figure 6.1 a diagram of how to conceptualize either early-onset cases that extend through adolescence or late-onset cases that begin at some point after puberty, either in adolescence or adulthood.

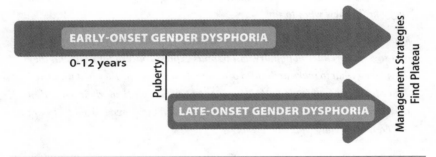

Figure 6.1. Early- and late-onset gender dysphoria

Early-onset cases used to be the more common presentation when we look at gender dysphoria (Yarhouse, 2015). They were more common among natal males than natal females at a ratio of as high as 4:1 or 5:1 at specialty clinics (Zucker, 2020b). Late-onset cases have actually become the more common clinical presentation in the past several years (Yarhouse & Sadusky, 2020; Zucker, 2020b). Also noteworthy, late-onset cases tend to be more common today among natal females than natal males. So the field has seen a flip in both sex ratio (more natal females than natal males) and in onset (more late- than early-onset). There is no current consensus as to why this is the case. There are certainly competing theories regarding late-onset cases. Some professionals view these cases as a result of societal acceptance of the transgender experience itself, while others are more critical of sociocultural shifts and peer-group influences through which needs for identity and community may be met by adopting a transgender identity. As we explained in our previous work (see Yarhouse & Sadusky, 2020, where we discuss the concept of "a looping effect" surrounding gender-identity diagnoses), we do not see either of these accounts as offering an adequate explanation for all of what we see in specialty clinics today.[1] We do not know what is contributing to the shift in onset and course, but we suspect that there are many variables at play. That being said, we advocate for continued research and examination of what might be contributing to these changes.

Recall that with early-onset cases the adolescent has experienced a persistence of their gender dysphoria. This experience has been a part of their life since childhood and has not resolved on its own as they went through puberty. They may experience more parental empathy for their present circumstances because their gender-atypical experiences throughout childhood were apparent to their family. Regarding the dysphoria itself, their experience of gender dysphoria may ebb and flow in severity, but it is unlikely to resolve now on its own, nor are there therapy protocols for resolving it with an adolescent's birth sex, which is in part why many people consider various strategies to manage their dysphoria, which we will cover in subsequent chapters.

Late-onset cases can be particularly challenging because parents often have no point of reference for the gender-identity questions their teen is raising. This can lead to tremendous skepticism on the part of some parents about any claims of gender dysphoria. This can be especially challenging if an adolescent is requesting more invasive procedures, such as hormone therapy (HT) or gender-confirmation surgery (GCS), particularly in cases where they have not yet undertaken a social transition.[2]

In both early- and late-onset cases, we work with the adolescent on identifying helpful management strategies and finding their "plateau," an analogy

---

[1]It should also be noted that with these competing theories we also see increased visibility of groups critical of current trends in care, especially the use of medical interventions for adolescents. See, for example, 4thWaveNow.com, "a community of people who question the medicalization of gender-atypical youth" (for a further discussion of these controversies in care, see Yarhouse & Sadusky, 2020).

[2]Indeed, Zucker (2020b) offers the following with respect to late-onset cases: "It is not clear whether this late-onset group should be deemed ineligible for early hormonal therapy or at least require some period of 'watchful waiting' or psychotherapy prior to making a decision about biomedical treatment" (p. 411).

we will explain in greater detail in chapter fourteen. This idea of a plateau versus mountaintop approach to exploring gender identity is that most adolescents come to believe that adopting a cross-gender or other gender identity through the use of HT or GCS is the "mountaintop" that they should all aspire to. That being said, we explain that a plateau is where we find many teens (and adults) who end up finding ways to manage their dysphoria that are creative and unique to each person but often do not entail medical interventions. We want to support teens in finding their plateau, with various landing points available to them. This honors the stepwise approach we take to managing gender dysphoria and recognizes that a plateau may be sufficient for a time, even if a person moves from it to other steps in the future.

HELICOPTERS AND AIRPLANES

An experience we have seen all too often in cases that might be described as late-onset gender dysphoria among natal females is a sense of urgency for invasive procedures. We have consulted with many teens who want what they want when they want it, which is often right away or as soon as a procedure for hormonal therapy and a surgery can be scheduled. This can result in points of tension when considering the 2011 WPATH standards, which recommend being on hormonal therapy for at least a year (in cases of using feminizing hormones) prior to seeking breast augmentation surgery. We can honor that many parents and many clients themselves will want to ensure that the decisions made here are done with reflection rather than hastiness, especially since the field lacks longitudinal outcome research that provides well-documented information about the risks and outcomes of hormonal therapies in transgender people (Firek & Sawan-Garcia, 2018). We want to acknowledge that these are not minor interventions; rather, these are urgent requests for procedures like chest-reconstruction surgery, for instance.

After seeing several such presentations, the image that came to mind was that of a helicopter ready to take off. It is as though the teen is a helicopter wanting to go straight up to reach altitude right away. In this analogy, altitude represents the hormone therapy or other interventions a teen wishes to take or the chest-reconstruction surgery the teen wishes to schedule. But we continued to observe that many of the parents are not in that same helicopter. Rather, to continue with this image, it's as though the parents are sitting in an airplane on the tarmac and just wondering what is going on as they listen to their teen discuss with urgency what they want.

This has been an interesting image to reflect on for several reasons. Not only does it capture the sense of urgency, but it also allows for a contrast in the experiences of the parents and their loved one. Also, we've learned from helicopter pilots that helicopters actually only rarely go straight up. Helicopters actually go forward into what might be thought of as a "zone of safety," and then up. If it's an emergency, a pilot can take a helicopter straight up, but the ideal takeoff for a helicopter is actually to go forward into this zone of safety and then up. What we have appreciated about learning about zones of safety is that this is an important part of the illustration to share with a teen. This image can also offer an opportunity to discuss the research that indicates that hormonal therapies have been found to be safe with adults when their provider is experienced in this space and actively monitoring their patient's progression, much like air traffic control would do (Weinand & Safer, 2015). We are not at this moment reaching the conclusion that what the teen is asking for is off the table, but we are asking about a safety zone, a way of moving forward that keeps the teenager's well-being in view and works with them, their parents, and others to find the best direction and the best timing for that direction.

With late-onset cases, we try to space out care so that we can determine that the experiences of reported dysphoria meet the criteria for the diagnosis of Gender Dysphoria (a minimum of six months). This also allows us to track the experiences and ebb and flow of dysphoria, as well as broader gender identity and how that relates to a person's religious identity over a span of time.

Generally speaking, we recommend that co-occurring issues such as depression and anxiety are addressed so that a person is not making decisions about gender identity through the lens of either a severe depression or anxious mood state. These and other mental or physical health concerns may present challenges to using hormones effectively (Sloan & Safer, 2018). Addressing co-occurring issues first has to be balanced, of course, against the consideration that the symptoms that look like depression or anxiety may be due to the gender-identity concerns.

Zucker (2020b) offers a helpful reflection on ways to think about co-occurring concerns. Mental health professionals may need to determine if gender dysphoria is present but related to a more primary mental health concern:

> In some instances, it may be that the [gender dysphoria] has emerged as secondary to another, more "primary" psychiatric disorder, such as autism spectrum disorder or borderline personality disorder, or as a result of a severe trauma

(e.g., sexual abuse). In such situations, it could be argued that the [gender dysphoria] would dissipate if the more primary condition were treated. (p. 411)

When we are concerned about disorders such as autism spectrum disorder (ASD), we try whenever possible to work with experts in both gender dysphoria and ASD who can share their expertise and offer recommendations for how to understand the relationship between the two.[3]

It is also possible that co-occurring mental health concerns could make it difficult to move forward with specific forms of care: "In other instances, it could be that the presence of other psychopathology (e.g., substance abuse) would interfere with the adolescent's ability to adhere to a biomedical treatment and there would be risks in trying to institute a regimen of hormonal therapy until stabilization is achieved" (Zucker, 2020b, p. 411).

But it is also possible for some symptoms to be the result of gender dysphoria or issues associated with gender dysphoria:

Last, there is the thorny issue regarding the extent to which the presence of other psychopathology (e.g., depression, suicidality) is due to the stress of having [gender dysphoria] or is secondary to the social ostracism and rejection that results from it. . . . On this point, one could argue that institution of treatment of [gender dysphoria] may reduce the secondary psychopathology. (Zucker, 2020b, p. 411)

When co-occurring concerns are present, it is important to carefully assess onset and course of gender dysphoria and any co-occurring issues so we can determine how to conceptualize gender dysphoria and its relationship to these other concerns, as well as how best to proceed.

The work of therapy, then, involves ongoing assessment, exploration, and consideration of the various factors at play. For many youth and families we have met with, the sense of urgency is real. It is important to help families appreciate how ongoing therapy can assist in peeling back the various layers here, and ultimately help youth and their families be more equipped to take whatever steps they deem appropriate moving forward. Therapy can be frustrating, in that few insights or clarifications happen overnight. Still, we find the work in therapy to be invaluable in helping youth as they seek effective treatment of gender dysphoria and any other difficulties they are facing. We now turn to the range of interventions that can assist you in this work.

---

[3]This is in keeping with recommendations from a recent Delphi study. See Strang et al., 2018.

7

THE JOURNEY TO FIND "ME"

Heather came to therapy to explore gender identity. She had disordered eating that she felt was exacerbated by gender dysphoria. Her eating disorder reduced her distress around secondary sex characteristics and kept her from experiencing her menstrual period. She was becoming more aware that the eating disorder functioned as a means of managing dysphoria she had experienced since childhood. In our first session, she fought back tears as she tried to explain a Trans+ support group she had attended the day before. The conversation had been about the name and pronouns each person identified with. "I am so sick of not knowing the answer to that," said Heather. "Some days, I can't stand hearing my name. Other times, it doesn't really bother me. But I don't know another option for me yet. I hate feeling this way, and I hate not knowing what will help."

What does it look like for mental health counselors to guide clients through questions of self-discovery? In a culture where gender-identity exploration, labeling, and advocacy are at the forefront of many young people's minds, those who struggle to decide how they want to identify may feel shame about their uncertainty. Consider Heather's story: since childhood, she had wished at times to be a boy—and at other times, she felt as if she already was one. After years of ignoring these questions, she was beginning to see how much gender-identity distress was impacting her life and perpetuating her eating disorder.

During counseling, it helped Heather to normalize her uncertainty by recognizing that people of all ages are navigating gender identity. She had initially felt far behind her peers in the process of self-discovery; it relieved her to know that we have met with people as old as seventy-five who were just beginning to find clarity about their gender dysphoria and how to manage it. We also validated the self-awareness that had prepared Heather to begin exploring her gender dysphoria more deeply. It is brave to explore such painful questions at any age, but Heather benefited from reassurance that there was no better time than the present to undertake this journey.

Heather's story highlights one of the challenges for those with gender dysphoria today. Since not everyone navigating gender identity experiences distress around their gender, many clients we have worked with feel isolated even from the transgender community, experiencing pressure to "have things figured out" before they truly belong. They long for space to ask important and difficult questions, and they will often look to individual therapy, in addition to or in place of peer contexts, to provide this space. Clients need a place where they can explore their questions without a fixed outcome and receive ongoing validation that they are not alone.

In this section of the book, we turn our attention to several counseling tools we have found helpful with adolescents and adults like Heather. We do not use each counseling tool with each client, nor do we necessarily use them in order. Rather, we incorporate them into counseling as needed to address pressing questions related to our overall case conceptualization and treatment plan. Our experience has been that once gender dysphoria persists through late adolescence (in early-onset cases), it does not tend to resolve on its own. As a field, we know much less about late-onset cases, but the tools we recommend here may still be useful in such cases. The next several chapters will focus on responding to experiences of enduring gender dysphoria while recognizing that some of the same principles can apply in cases where dysphoria has only recently been observed.

VIEWING POLARITIES

One counseling tool we tend to incorporate into the early stages of counseling is referred to as "The Journey to Find 'Me.'" In this exercise, we invite our client to help us better understand how they currently experience gender-identity questions or concerns. We do this by asking them to visually depict their goals for gender identity along a continuum between different polarities. Since we know that people experience gender-related distress in a range of ways, this exercise helps clients define for themselves what they are currently experiencing and how they hope this experience will evolve over time.

What do we mean by polarities? Polarities are two opposite aspects of a person's experience of gender identity. While we want the client to select their own list of terms, we have found it helpful to begin by listing several terms commonly used by other clients exploring gender identity and faith. These common terms are shown in figure 7.1. We have met with people for whom one or more of these polarities resonates for one reason or another. A client can select as many as resonate with them.

Pain?	Pleasure?
Sickness?	Healing?
Dysphoria?	No/less dysphoria?
Conflict?	Peace?
Fallenness?	Redemption?
Shame?	Pride?
Weakness?	Strength?
Confusion?	Clarity?
Despair?	Hope?

Figure 7.1. Terms to describe the experience of gender identity

You will note in worksheet 7.1 that the client is prompted to locate themselves along a continuum between these various polarities. For many people, identifying where they fall along a continuum between polarities becomes an initial way to think about themselves, their conflict, and the direction they wish to move.

Most people feel that their goal should be to move away from pain and toward pleasure, from the left side of the continuum toward the right. You can remind your client that *pleasure* will mean different things to different people; it may be helpful to unpack what the word means to your client. Some people find pleasure in fulfilling work, education, time with loved ones, and so on. But we recognize that what is pleasurable may vary considerably from person to person.

Even the act of choosing which polarities to address can be an important process of self-discovery for clients. It is fairly common for people to mark the continuum with the terms that represent their own most unpleasant experiences and the ideals they believe will satisfy them most.

The primary purpose of this tool is to help the client reflect on their journey. Does their path lead away from the experience of dysphoria? Do they anticipate that this internal sense of incongruence will stop completely at some point along their journey? Perhaps sufficient resolution will be found somewhere along the continuum (and this point of resolution will vary from client to client). Regardless, we believe the focus of therapy should be on the journey, not the ending.

In chapter eight, we will invite our clients to reflect further on the question of who they are. For now, we want to provide our client with an opportunity to define "me" for themselves.

For people of faith, the question "Who am I?" is often heavily influenced by their understanding of who God is and his plan for their lives. Absolute autonomy over one's identity is not a concept heavily emphasized in Christianity. In fact, many Christians denounce the possibility of asking "Who am I?" apart from first asking how God sees them. Some people of faith appreciate us acknowledging that their self-definition can be considered in the context of how they believe God sees them. At the same time, if the question "Who am I?" is only ever addressed in terms of how clients have been told by others that God sees them, they may find it difficult to ever arrive at a personal identity that is both personally honest and consistent with their beliefs.

Observing myself and my world. Many people we work with do not realize the ways self-stigma informs their perspective of their own gender dysphoria and the dysphoria of others they encounter. Self-stigma is defined as "the reduction in a person's self-esteem or sense of self-worth due to the perception held by the individual that he or she is socially unacceptable" (Vogel et al., 2013, p. 312). Clinical interventions around self-stigma can help a person build a sense of self-efficacy and value even if public perceptions of the person do not change.

One valuable early intervention is to have clients take stock of how they see others who experience gender dysphoria and how this perception is different from or similar to the way they see themselves in this process. We often begin this conversation with two preliminary questions:

- How do I feel about people who experience gender dysphoria? What do I think of them?

- How do I feel about the fact that I experience gender dysphoria? What do I think of myself?

After these preliminary questions, we explore how a client reacts to themselves in their experience of gender dysphoria. The distinction between the next set of questions and the last is important; these next questions move beyond cognitive and affective observation *of* the self, into personal reactions and relationship *to* the self:

- In what way does it scare me to experience gender dysphoria? What makes it scary for me?

- In what way does it excite me to experience gender dysphoria? What makes it exciting for me?

- What other words would I use to describe how I feel about my sense of gender dysphoria?

We can then delve deeper still. Moving beyond the felt experience of gender dysphoria, clients benefit from being asked to reflect on their deepest inclinations toward their gender identity. We use the language of *parts* in these questions in order to call attention to the aspects of clients' inclinations that may reside beneath the surface:

- Is there a part of me that feels bad or condemned about my experiences of gender identity? What part and why?

- Is there a part of me that feels concerned or confused about my experiences of gender identity? What part and why?

- Is there a part of me that feels okay, neutral, or good about my experiences of gender identity? What part and why?

Exploration of various aspects of identity. The clients we see place a high importance on many aspects of their identity. There is no way of knowing at the outset which aspects of identity most inform their personhood, decisions, and current challenges. Thus, a significant focus of early therapy is to honor and appreciate the range of aspects of client identity. This is especially true when we work with adolescents, who can be prone to foreclose some aspects of their identity or to hyperfocus on certain aspects to the exclusion of others.

Chris is a seventeen-year-old natal female who presents to group therapy at an outpatient eating-disorder clinic. On her first day of therapy, Chris sits down and announces to the group, "Hi, I am genderfluid." The facilitator notices that several of Chris's peers chime in, naming their gender-identity labels as well. The therapist makes note that gender identity is an important aspect of these adolescents' identity. However, the therapist also helps individuals share other aspects of themselves without feeling as if the only important aspect of their identity is gender identity in every case.

It is increasingly evident that young people today are drawn to emerging gender identities more readily than previous generations have been. Of course, emerging gender-identity categories, such as bigender, aporagender, demigender, feminine-of-center, graygender, and so on, have developed relatively recently, meaning that this generation of youth is the first to go through adolescence aware of such categories. These youth benefit from being able to "thicken the plot" for themselves and their family members about who they are, both as gendered people and as holistic people. Yet the significance of these new categories to many youths' identities by no means supplants the significance of other identities. According to the APA, "even when gender identity is the main focus of care, psychologists are encouraged to understand that a [transgender or gender-nonconforming] person's experience of gender may also be shaped by other important aspects of identity (e.g., age, race/ethnicity, sexual orientation), and that the salience of different aspects of identity may evolve as the person continues psychosocial development across the lifespan, regardless of whether they complete a social or medical transition" (APA, 2015, p. 837).

A helpful initial exercise here, in addition to understanding "me" as it relates to gender identity, can be for the client to outline aspects of their identity that are important to and inform their sense of self. For example, the client could draw a large circle on a piece of paper, writing various words inside it that symbolize important aspects of their identity. They could also draw circles of varying sizes around each word to convey the weight of this aspect of identity or its relative importance to their personhood.

Here are sample journaling questions that some clients have found helpful:

- If I had to describe myself (my identity) in a few sentences, what would I say?
- What are some of the parts of me that I find most important?
- What are some roles I would like to have during my lifetime?
- What part of my identity (if any) does my gender identity play right now?
- What are the ways my experience of gender identity helps me explore other aspects of my identity? What are the ways my experience of gender identity complicates my exploration of other aspects of my identity?

Given these questions' focus on a range of aspects of identity, this phase of exploration can also be an opportunity for clients to appreciate the impact of religious/cultural identity on their gendered experience. A client's important beliefs and values often emerge at this point; they can begin to name the role of religion/spirituality in their sense of identity and the ways this aspect of identity complicates or clarifies their journey of gender-identity exploration. By considering the weight they give to their beliefs and values, as well as to other aspects of their identity, a client can gain insight into the relevant factors in their journey. Understanding the intersection of identity variables can also help to foster resilience when those identities come in conflict (APA, 2015, p. 837; Singh, 2013).

We want to emphasize your role as the clinician in supporting clients' exploration of their faith and other aspects of identity. The APA (2010) ethics code, which governs our work as psychologists, is clear about the need to be sensitive to, aware of, and respectful toward all individual differences. These include religious beliefs, values, and practices that could inform someone's identity. Many people of faith are hesitant to bring up their faith in therapy, and many therapists report feeling ill equipped to address it (Hathaway et al., 2004). In our work with clients, the integration of various aspects of identity is paramount. Thus, we want to reiterate the importance of showing cultural sensitivity to all aspects of identity and listening to the priorities and perspectives of clients. In fact, the APA cautions against providers overemphasizing gender identity and expression when these are "not directly relevant" to the client's concerns (APA, 2015, p. 836).

Another matter clinicians must consider is the way power and privilege—or stigma and disempowerment—emerge at the intersection of various identities. According to recent APA guidelines for working with transgender clients, intersectionality may impact a person's access to resources and social support (APA, 2015, p. 837). A similar dynamic is likely at play when individuals experience conflict between religious identity and gender identity. Notably, researchers have found that positive relationships with faith community leaders are important for the maintenance of personal faith in the midst of exploring and consolidating a gender identity (Glaser, 2008; Porter et al., 2013; Xavier, 2000). As clinicians we can encourage clients to attend to complexities of which they may be unaware in order to maximize their well-being.

WORKING WITH FAMILIES

It is often helpful to remind parents and other family members that, even as their loved one explores emerging aspects of their gender identity, the loved one is still the same person. We have found that family members can become hyperfocused on gender identity, as if this identity changes or negates everything else they know about their loved one.

One tool that has been especially useful to parents involves taking a blank sheet of paper and writing on one half a list of all the qualities they have come to know and appreciate about their loved one. Parents often mention their loved one's intelligence or sense of humor, commitment to Christ, loyalty to friends, and so on. Once these qualities are written on half of the paper, we draw a line to split the paper in two and write on the other half, "Your child's gender-identity exploration." Their child's gender-identity questions, we suggest, do not negate all the qualities listed on the other side of the line. Indeed, if parents are just now learning about their child's gender-identity questions, these questions present an opportunity for parents to know their children better. After all, children have often been navigating these questions for some time before sharing with their parents. This exercise can serve as a concrete reminder to families that what they have learned about gender identity is simply another aspect of their loved one, not a revelation that negates everything else they know about their loved one.

We want to close this chapter by noting the value of narrative as you begin work with clients navigating gender identity. One of the primary purposes of narrative therapy, developed by Michael White and David Epston, is to help clients distinguish themselves as whole people from their current difficulties so that they can experience greater clarity and autonomy. The narrative model invites clients to see their life experiences as parts of a broader personal story (Morgan, 2000). Clients are then positioned to author that story to some extent—or, as many people of faith understand it, to act as a coauthor of the story they see God writing for their life. We suggest that clients consider their lives as divided into various chapters (a strategy we will discuss more explicitly later).

Thinking about life in this way, as a book with many chapters, allows clients not only to write new chapters but also to edit previous chapters over time. After all, this initial reflection on the journey to finding "me" is just that:

an initial reflection as part of a broader journey. Some people we have met with are afraid that if they establish a sense of self now and give a name to that sense, they will be tied down to it later. The unpredictability of an unknown future can paralyze clients from ever reflecting on where they are now. We want our clients to know that they need not be tied down by their past self-concept any more than by their current one. The chapters they narrate in therapy merely give us a chance to appreciate where they are today; these chapters will be subject to change, not only over the course of therapy but over the course of their lives.

WORKSHEET 7.1. THE JOURNEY TO FIND "ME"

Directions: Take a look at the image below of lines running from left to right. On the first one we marked the far left with the word *pain* and the far right with the word *pleasure*; just above the middle, we wrote the word *Me*.

The lines represent a continuum—a range from one extreme to the other.

Circle the words (you can select more than one) that represent a way you see yourself or one of your goals for navigating gender identity and faith. Then indicate where you are currently between the words you have indicated are important to you by placing *Me* along that continuum between the words you have selected.

Me

Pain?	Pleasure?
Sickness?	Healing?
Dysphoria?	No/Less Dysphoria?
Conflict?	Peace?
Fallenness?	Redemption?
Shame?	Pride?
Weakness?	Strength?
Confusion?	Clarity?
Despair?	Hope?

Many people want their "me" to move along the continuum from left to right, away from pain and toward pleasure. *Pleasure*, of course, will mean different things to different people. Some people find pleasure in fulfilling work, education, time with loved ones, and so on. But we recognize that what is pleasurable may vary considerably from person to person.

Below the terms *pain* and *pleasure* we have marked the continuum with other opposing terms like *sickness* and *healing*; *dysphoria* and *no/less dysphoria*; *conflict* and *peace*. You may want to mark the continuum with the terms that represent your own most unpleasant experiences on one side and what you believe will most satisfy you on the other side.

Does your path lead away from the experience of dysphoria? Do you anticipate that this internal sense of incongruence will stop completely at some point during your journey? Or are you simply hoping to find sufficient resolution somewhere along the continuum? Regardless of where you hope your "me" is moving, we encourage you to focus on the journey, not the ending.

We will talk more in later sessions about what it means to learn who you are. In the meantime, how would you define "me" for yourself?

_____

_____

_____

Reflect on the following question: Does your path lead to peace with family, friends, yourself, and even God?

_____

_____

_____

While we hope that you sense peace in all your relationships (including your relationship with God), we believe there can be little lasting peace if you do not have a sense of "me."

Focusing on the outcome you hope for (that is, the far right side of the continuum) can put a lot of unnecessary pressure on you as you try to understand your path forward and to define your real self. There is no shame in recognizing where you are right now and admitting to yourself what your current experience is like.

Also, we recognize that using a single continuum line may be too limiting. You may wish to write one word on the left from which multiple lines run to many possible outcomes on the right. After all, there are multiple paths you can take, and these paths can lead to multiple discoveries about your real self and multiple destinations.

Notes:

_____

_____

_____

_____

8

A MULTITIER DISTINCTION

AN ADDITIONAL TOOL often introduced in the early stages of counseling explores gender identity by distinguishing between descriptive and prescriptive approaches to gender (sometimes framed as the difference between "how I am" and "who I am").[1] This tool also invites clients to consider the different language available to them for self-description ("I am transgender" or "I am a transgender person" or "I am a person who experiences gender dysphoria") and what these different terms may mean to themselves and others.

As clients think about their gender, they may find it helpful to reflect on how they will describe their experiences or what label they will adopt to name their reality. In other words, they may decide to say, "I'm a person who experiences gender dysphoria" or "I am a person exploring gender identity" instead of "I am transgender" or "I am gender nonbinary." For some clients, the first two labels may feel descriptive while the latter two may feel prescriptive of particular pathways; other clients may feel that words like *trans* simply describe their dysphoria and do not dictate their relationship to their birth sex or steps they will take to manage dysphoria. Regardless, thinking carefully about labels will allow clients to take stock of the many factors contributing to their understanding of gender, the many people (including themselves) responsible for interpreting those factors, and the benefits (and costs) of ignoring, accepting, or altering any given factor.

THE POWER OF A LABEL

We want to invite our clients to consider how they wish to use language, particularly as they are exploring gender identity. We invite them to explore the power of labels in light of the idea that a linguistic identity is often the endpoint

---

[1]This approach was first introduced in Yarhouse, 2015, pp. 136-37.

of a process of identity discernment. Some clients prefer to avoid labels, describing their gender-diverse experience (to themselves and others) without utilizing a common label; others prefer labels as helpful ways to convey (again, to themselves and to others) their experience of gender identity.

A client may wonder, "Since I experience gender dysphoria, doesn't that make me transgender?" Well, not necessarily. People have many options for describing themselves and their experiences in light of gender-identity questions:

1. Some people choose to avoid the term *transgender* by describing themselves as "someone who experiences gender dysphoria" or "someone who is exploring questions around gender identity."

2. Some people are comfortable using terms like *transgender* or *gender nonbinary* but prefer to do so only in certain ways, describing themselves as "someone who is transgender" or "someone who is gender nonbinary." (Those who do so may feel that this grammatical construction makes the label descriptive rather than prescriptive; they are describing their experience of *how* they are rather than asserting *who* they are.)

3. Some people choose to use labels like *trans*, whether descriptively or prescriptively, in their simplest grammatical form: "I am transgender." (For a subset of this group, this phrasing signifies the adoption of a prescriptive transgender identity, indicating not just *how* they are but also *who* they are.)

The client you are meeting with may see a term like *transgender* or *gender nonbinary* as a label that carries an entire culture with it. If the client is reluctant to adopt all of the term's cultural implications for themselves, they may wish to say, "I am someone who experiences gender dysphoria" or "I am someone who is exploring questions of gender identity" and elect not to say "I am transgender" or "I am gender nonbinary."

Some clients may feel comfortable adopting a label to describe themselves and their experiences, even if that label sometimes includes cultural assumptions the client wishes to reject. In such cases, the client's use of the label in conversation with others may cause them to be misperceived by others. Even if the client finds a certain label convenient or helpful for their own self-understanding, some of their friends or acquaintances may assume that terms like *transgender* or other emerging gender-identity labels are inextricably linked to entire systems of culture and belief. That is, some people may hear your client use the term *transgender* about themselves and then assign all sorts of cultural expectations to their simple use of a label.

Other clients with gender dysphoria or clients exploring gender identity use the label *transgender* for themselves precisely because they agree with the cultural assumptions the term sometimes carries. For these clients, adopting a transgender identity serves to indicate their alignment with a certain cultural or belief system. It is important for clinicians to understand—and to help their clients understand—what kind of impact an identity label might be performing in a client's self-conception.

There is a lot of power in labels, after all.

When someone begins to label themselves, they often begin to behave in ways consistent with that category. Labels can help people identify new ways to think about themselves, their experiences, and even their history in light of a wide range of linguistic constructs.

Ian Hacking (1995) describes a "looping effect" in which people interact with the categories used to account for their experiences. That is, the language people use to describe themselves—and the language available to them as they decide *how* to describe themselves—tends to shape the way in which people evaluate and interact with their own experience. When we apply Hacking's principle to individuals exploring gender-identity questions, we can see the significance of how linguistic categories have developed over the course of history to describe the experiences now known as diverse gender identities. Previously prominent terms like *transsexual, transvestic, gender-identity dis-ordered*, and *gender dysphoric* have all informed the self-understanding of those they described. When people navigating gender identity interacted with these categories and expressed their preference to be known publicly and politically as transgender, this new category of self-understanding eventually paved the way for additional accounts of gender-identity experience, including emerging gender identities such as gender nonbinary, genderfluid, bigender, agender, gender expansive, and gender creative.

Instead of talking about having a transgender, gender-nonbinary, or other identity, some clients find it helpful to depict their experience in more descriptive terms. For these clients, descriptive terminology frees them from others' expectations for how they will behave, present, or express their gender identity. Descriptive language has also helped some clients talk in detail about their gender dysphoria: its intensity and duration (how strong the dysphoria is, when it spikes or diminishes, how long a spike lasts, and so on) as well as what events or relationships or experiences make the dysphoria stronger.

There can be advantages to purely descriptive language.

At the same time, being descriptive can hold some elements of a person's identity at arm's length. While this sense of separation can be useful for making sober evaluations, descriptive language may not be sustainable if a person feels they must indefinitely hold elements of their identity at a distance. The avoidance of labels can indicate a person's increasingly deferred hope that their gender dysphoria will abate, a hope that they will be "cured" or "fixed" or "healed" in ways that may not be realistic. Label avoidance can also feel reductionistic. Although people are often told to use descriptive language in order to escape the danger of becoming too focused on their gender identity, they sometimes find that purely descriptive language draws attention to itself and so places even more focus on their gender identity. On the other hand, adopting common identity labels makes it easier for some clients to move past their fixation with language and focus on other aspects of their experience. Over time, many people gravitate toward adopting language and identity labels that reflect a balanced acceptance of their gender identity (see worksheet 8.1).

When we work with people trying to find their way forward in gender-identity exploration, they may find it helpful for a season to use purely descriptive language. They may also elect to use language that falls between plain description ("I am a person who is navigating gender identity") and plain use of a label ("I am transgender") by saying something like "I am someone who is transgender" or "I am a transgender person." These clients may feel that using the word *transgender* in such sentences describes part of their experience without characterizing the whole. They are simply describing *how* they are—that *transgender* or *gender nonbinary* or another term depicts part of their reality—rather than asserting that this identity represents the whole of who they are. They may feel that this language allows them to describe their gender experience without carrying over an entire culture of meanings.

A client can also use the term *transgender* (or any other term for their gender experience) and immediately share their personal definition of the term. This approach may work best for clients in a later portion of their journey. For example, a person might say, "I consider myself to be transgender—that is, I am someone who _____." They might then go on to explain their own current approach to gender questions, perhaps by using descriptive words such as "searching" or "thinking it through." In addition, they might choose to clarify how they live out their gender, perhaps by sharing an area of their life (such as clothing or relationships) where this personal definition of *transgender* influences their actions.

People who adopt this strategy for a season tend to define their key terms quickly and may elect to use words like "currently" to allow room for change in the future. As with the previous approach, some clients may find this approach helpful for conveying who they are and how they live. Specifically, it provides an opportunity for clients to clarify to others how they may resonate with some parts of the transgender label even as they distance themselves from aspects of transgender culture more broadly. Again, this approach may fit some clients well at various points in their journey.

MORE REFLECTION ON THE HOW I AM AND WHO I AM DISTINCTION

A related exercise that might be helpful for your clients is to reflect on whether they view gender dysphoria as *how* a person is or *who* a person is, a distinction we introduced at the beginning of this chapter. This distinction may not resonate with everyone who experiences gender dysphoria, but some have found it useful.

If someone were to ask your client, "How are you?," they would most likely reply with, "I feel well" or "I am a bit sick." Feeling well (or being a bit sick) is most likely *not* part of your client's intrinsic and deep-seated sense of identity. A person could even have a very serious condition like diabetes or cancer while recognizing that they are not just a diabetic or a cancer patient. They are more than how they feel or what their diagnosis is.

If someone were to ask your client, "Who are you?," they would most likely reply with, "My name is Sally, and I am a student at the university" or "My name is Tom, and I work over at that department store." To some degree, their name is part of their intrinsic identity, but where they attend college or work is most often *not* part of their intrinsic identity.

If someone were to ask your client, "What are you?," they would probably stare in silence, unsure how to answer such an awkward question. If they did answer the question, they might reply with answers that gesture toward their deep and intrinsic identity: "I am a country boy, not a city person" or "I am a lover of hip-hop music" or "I am an American of Scottish descent."

However, imagine that someone were to ask your client this fourth question: "No, I don't mean any of those things. What I mean is this: Who are you at your deepest level?" Your client now knows the questioner is not asking for something superficial but wants to understand their deep and intrinsic sense of self—their identity.

Clients may find it helpful to evaluate their answers to all these questions by drawing a clear distinction between *how* and *who*. For this purpose, let *how* signify those things your client experiences that *are not* part of their deep internal sense of self. *Who*, by contrast, can signify those parts of your client's identity that are very deep and that they experience as intrinsic.

When defined this way, *how* and *who* represent two diverging ways in which people who experience gender dysphoria may view their experiences. Thinking in terms of *how* and *who* may help clients gain perspective on their journey. Your client can complete worksheet 8.2 to explore this distinction for themselves.

Keep in mind that the distinction between who you are and how you are is not for everyone. It may or may not resonate with your client. If the distinction seems artificial or otherwise does not resonate, don't use it. Your client may also find it helpful for a season but not for the rest of their life. It may be that they will arrive at a more fixed sense of identity after a process of identity discernment. This distinction between *who* and *how* may be helpful during the discernment phase if the descriptive language it fosters can give your client the space they need to think through their experiences for themselves.

We also want to acknowledge that people may identify differently in private from how they identify publicly. A private identity is what a person sees when they look in the mirror. A public identity is who a person is known to be by others. The relationship between these two identities can be complicated for some people navigating gender identity. They may experience distress because of the incongruity between the way they are known (or want to be known) publicly and the way they see themselves (or are beginning to see themselves) privately. The distinction between public and private identity is an important one and underscores the conflict some people feel around gender identity.

This conflict can take a variety of forms. Tim, a natal male exploring gender identity, saw himself as a male privately but was beginning to wish he could be known publicly as agender or gender queer. When he noticed in our session one day that he privately referred to himself as male, he became disgruntled. "How can I expect anyone to see me any other way if I refer to myself as male, despite the pain it causes me?!" Introducing the distinction between public and private identities can make space for people like Tim to understand how they might see themselves differently from how they want others to see them. Conversely to Tim's story, a person might identify privately as transgender or gender nonbinary but publicly present as cisgender. In such cases, the difference between the person's public and private identities may have to do with safety concerns about disclosing their private identity to others, feelings of shame about presenting differently in public, or a number of other factors.

As we bring this chapter to a close, we want to reiterate that your clients are more than their gender identity, regardless of how they describe themselves. A person's identity—their sense of self—is always more than their gender identity. At the same time, gender identity is an important aspect of personhood, and we want to be careful not to minimize its significance.

WORKSHEET 8.1. A MULTITIER DISTINCTION IN LANGUAGE AND MEANING

Directions: Consider the following multitier distinction in language and meaning around gender dysphoria and identity. Tier 1 describes your experience without using an identity label. Tier 2 uses the label *transgender* but creates distance between the adjective and the person it describes; for some clients, this phrasing might signify a description of *how* they are rather than *who* they are. Tier 3 uses *transgender* as an identity label without putting distance between the adjective and the person; for some clients, this phrasing might signify a description of *who* they are rather than *how* they are. Tier 4 uses *transgender* but then offers an account of what the term means to you.

A Multitier Distinction in Language and Meaning

	LANGUAGE	MEANING
Tier 1	"I am a person who experiences gender dysphoria."	A descriptive way to convey part of your experience without using a label.
Tier 2	"I am someone who is transgender" or "I am a transgender person."	Added distance between adjective and person; may convey *how* you are rather than *who* you are.
Tier 3	"I am transgender."	No added distance between adjective and person; may convey *who* you are rather than *how* you are.
Tier 4	"I am transgender, which I define as . . ."	Use of *transgender* and a personal definition to more accurately convey both *who* and *how* you are.

(*Adapted with permission from Yarhouse, 2015, p. 137.*)

1. Have you seen this distinction before? Does it make sense to you? Is it helpful in understanding your experiences? If so, how? What questions do you have about it?

_____

_____

_____

_____

_____

2. What language/labels have you used previously? Has this language differed based on audience or circumstances?

_____

_____

_____

_____

_____

3. What might be the potential benefits and drawbacks to using descriptive language for your experiences while avoiding identity labels?

_____

_____

_____

_____

_____

4. What might be the potential benefits and drawbacks to using identity labels (e.g., "I am transgender" or "I am gender nonbinary")?

_____

_____

_____

_____

_____

5. Are you currently using any labels to describe your experience? Do these differ with regard to how you identify privately versus how you identify publicly?

_____

_____

_____

_____

_____

_____

WORKSHEET 8.2. HOW I AM / WHO I AM DISTINCTION

Directions: Please journal your thoughts in the table below, as you reflect on the distinction between *how* you are and *who* you are.

MAKING A DISTINCTION

HOW I AM	WHO I AM
What experiences have you had, or what messages have you received, that tell you your experiences of gender dysphoria or gender identity are *how* you are?	What experiences have you had, or what messages have you received, that tell you your experiences of gender dysphoria or gender identity are *who* you are?
What do you like about thinking of your gender dysphoria or gender identity as how you are?	What do you like about thinking of your gender dysphoria or gender identity as who you are?
What questions do you have about the language or wording of "how you are"?	What questions do you have about the language or wording of "who you are"?

9

IDENTIFYING SCRIPTS
AND STORYLINES

SCRIPTS REFER TO CULTURAL EXPECTATIONS for how people behave and relate to one another (Yarhouse, 2010; 2015). There are scripts for all kinds of behaviors. For example, there are cultural expectations for how people greet one another, and these scripts are different for family, close friends, or acquaintances. There are cultural expectations for how people depart from one another—again, these scripts differ according to relationship, circumstances, and so on. People also have cultural expectations for how we sit as an audience during an orchestral performance, as well as for significant life decisions such as when single persons should marry or when a couple should have children. These behaviors are not dictated by cultural expectations, but they are certainly influenced by them.

In a similar way, there are scripts for gender identity. These scripts are sometimes referred to as gender roles, gender stereotypes, and/or cultural expectations for what it means to be a boy or a girl, a man or a woman.

SCRIPTS AROUND SEX AND GENDER

As clients begin to explore their gender and what it means to them, they may find it helpful to sort through the messages they received growing up about what it means to be a man, a woman, or another gender identity. People easily absorb and internalize these messages, even without realizing they are doing so.

Some messages have to do with interests ("Men like to do _____; women like to do _____"). Other messages concern personality or temperament ("Men are this way while women are this other way; men's brains seem to have neural connections that lend toward _____ while women's brains are more suited for _____").

Still other messages focus on the purpose of a person's life, perhaps including marriage, family, or reproduction (e.g., the capacity of a woman to conceive and give birth to a child may be more meaningful to some people than to others).

We offer additional journaling questions here to explore some of these scripts:

- What messages have you received from others about what it means to be a man? To what extent would you describe these messages as healthy and accurate? Unhealthy and inaccurate?

- What messages have you received from others about what it means to be a woman? To what extent would you describe these messages as healthy and accurate? Unhealthy and inaccurate?

- What do you mean when you use the word *masculine*?

- What do you mean when you use the word *feminine*?

- As you reflect on what you have written about your own definition of *masculine* and *feminine*, how would you say your definition of these words is similar to or different from the messages you've received from others about what it means to be a man or a woman?

SCRIPTS AROUND GENDER DYSPHORIA

There is an emerging cultural script for making sense of gender identity when a person is diagnosed with Gender Dysphoria. This script may include any of the following:

- If you are experiencing gender dysphoria, then you are transgender in your identity and are part of the transgender community (however you or your culture defines that community).

- The transgender community is part of the larger LGBTQ+ community, which has emerged as a culture of its own in recent years.

- Dysphoria signals identity, pointing to something that is at the core of who you are; it is foundational to identity.

- You are born this way.

- Being transgender is your identity.

- If you experience gender dysphoria, it makes sense to pursue resolution of the dysphoria by living in a different gender role and/or by hormonal treatment and/or by gender-confirmation surgery.

Scripts become compelling insofar as they help a person make sense of what may be confusing or distressing for them. They can provide a sense of identity ("Who am I?") and a sense of community ("How am I similar to others?"). Some scripts also provide a sense of direction for the future ("I know what the future holds for me"), which can be very compelling and stabilizing when a person feels directionless.

At the same time, any particular script can limit options. Any script can limit questions and explorations. Any script can limit uniqueness, leading a person to foreclose on a potentially life-giving pathway.

Clients have sometimes been offered scripts because they experience gender dysphoria or because they identify as transgender. In some cases, their instinct may be to reach out for a script and accept it automatically— after all, a script gives some sense of identity, community, and direction.

However, one danger of accepting a script too quickly is that multitudes of scripts exist. Those who offer these scripts to one another are often familiar only with the script that worked for them. What if a client wishes to write their own script, at their own pace, with their own set of characters, with their own ad lib or improvisation along the way?

Very often, people of faith criticize a range of storylines without acknowledging that they are offering (or not offering) counterstorylines of their own. Many religious organizations are either silent about gender dysphoria or speak negatively about it. In either case, the way these organizations engage or disengage questions about gender identity creates scripts and sets of expectations for people navigating these issues.

One natal female who experiences gender dysphoria told us she encountered the following messages from conservative religious circles of which she was a part:

1. You have a moral obligation to behave like a "traditional woman," and anything else is just prideful self-assertion.

2. You will become truly authentic and self-fulfilled only if you adopt a traditional gender role.

3. Cross-gender behaviors are unacceptable because they are trying to undermine the truth about the human person made "in the image and likeness of God."

4. Gender dysphoria is a psychological disorder probably caused by homosexual behavior. You should go to therapy or into a ministry to fix or heal it.

5. You feel unhappy about your femininity because you feel unhappy about yourself as a person. Maybe if someone taught you how to do your makeup and helped you buy some really nice, flattering clothes for your body type, you'd be more confident.

Is there a primary conventionally religious script about gender identity that is communicated directly or indirectly to people who experience gender dysphoria or are navigating gender-identity questions? In our experience working with people navigating gender identity, we would describe a primary conservative (some might say ultraconservative) religious script saying something like this:

- The experience of gender incongruence is sin. You should confess and repent. (In some circles, gender incongruence may be deemed a psychological disorder rather than a spiritual disorder. In these instances, the message may be that the cause should be uncovered in ministry or counseling so that the person can experience healing.)

- You will become truly authentic and self-fulfilled as the result of adopting a gender identity corresponding to your natal sex and a traditional gender role.

- You feel displeased with your own masculinity or femininity because of sin or ingratitude. (In some circles, the displeasure is the result of feeling unhappy as a person.)

- Cross-gender behaviors or other gender identity expressions are unacceptable because they undermine the truth about the person being made by God as male or female.

These messages form scripts that communicate cultural expectations. Yet the narrative they tell is not the only narrative available to those who experience gender dysphoria. It is possible to be authentic without adopting a traditional gender role, to find wholeness without fitting into cultural expectations for being a traditional male or traditional female.

Cultural expectations can also pressure those who experience gender dysphoria in the other direction, toward transitioning. Yet, the scripts that communicate these expectations are no more comprehensive than the prevailing scripts of religious conservatism. It is possible to experience gender dysphoria and yet not identify as transgender, to find peace and fulfillment without transitioning socially or hormonally or surgically.

Each client is a complex person writing their own script. They are not obligated to follow any one script, whether that script comes from the mainstream LGBTQ+ community or is rooted in traditional gender roles.

Some people choose to define their experiences of gender identity or dysphoria in accordance with a given script because they are unaware of the existence of other scripts. It takes courage for a client to investigate the scripts they are given, to question these scripts, and to create their own unique script. We want to reflect this courage to our clients and invite them into a process of exploration.

What alternatives to the prevailing scripts for gender identity and gender dysphoria can clinicians offer to their clients? We refer to such alternative offerings as *other possible storylines* (fig. 9.2) that run contrary to the given *primary scripts* (fig. 9.1). These alternative stories provide alternative frameworks through which people who experience gender-identity questions or gender dysphoria can choose to view and understand their experiences.

Reading from these primary scripts has led some people to confuse "how I am" with "who I am," assuming that their experiences must give information about their deepest essence. For some people who experience gender-identity questions or gender dysphoria, a transgender identity may feel like the only choice until they hear about other alternatives.

Others experience their churches' scripts as limiting and self-destructive. Unable to fit into rigid gender stereotypes, they may feel guilty of a personal failure.

To help our clients identify whether and how these scripts have been part of their experiences, we invite them to complete worksheet 9.1 and worksheet 9.2. These worksheets ask clients to journal about the words, phrases, and stories they have heard about transgender and otherwise gender-diverse persons. If possible, clients should include both stories from their faith

PRIMARY TRANSGENDER SCRIPT	PRIMARY CONSERVATIVE RELIGIOUS SCRIPT
Experiencing gender dysphoria = trans or nonbinary identity (communicating "who I am").	Experiencing gender dysphoria = willful disobedience (sin) or a mental disorder that resulted from sinful behavior.
I belong to the transgender and gender-diverse culture (whatever I believe that may look like).	I belong to the Christian community provided I repent of sin (or go to a ministry for healing).
I was born this way.	I am making poor choices by being gender incongruent.
My incongruence and associated dysphoria signal something about the core of who I am; it signals something at the foundation of my identity.	I will become truly authentic and self-fulfilled only if I adopt a traditional gender role.
Being *transgender, nonbinary,* or otherwise *gender diverse* is the focus of my identity.	I have a moral obligation to behave like a "traditional woman" or a "traditional man," and anything else is just prideful self-assertion.
If I experience gender dysphoria, it makes sense to pursue resolution of the dysphoria only by living in a different gender role and/or only by hormonal treatment and/or only by gender-confirmation surgery.	Cross-gender behaviors are unacceptable because they are trying to undermine the truth about the human person made "in the image and likeness of God."

(Adapted with permission from Yarhouse, 2015, pp. 131-34.)

Figure 9.1. Competing scripts

community growing up and stories from the LGBTQ+ community, media, and entertainment. These contrasting stories may reflect different points of tension for clients.

In closing, we want to point out that some people who experience gender dysphoria read from the script they are given like an unskilled actor might do. They never question the lines they are quoting and adopting. In the end, their role becomes more like putting on an act, leaving them and others feeling that the execution of the script is hollow. After all, they are not truly the characters they portray; they are merely actors, mimicking a script without effort or without bringing their humanity and personhood into the script they have been given.

We want to help our clients recognize that they have many options available to them. Neither experiences of gender dysphoria nor general gender-identity questions force a person into a particular pathway. Likewise, these same experiences need not be combated with stricter gender roles. The storylines most prevalent in certain LGBTQ+ circles and conservative religious circles are not the *only* choices.

Figure 9.2 illustrates some ways other storylines read as compared to the primary scripts from the transgender community and from the conservative religious community.

OTHER POSSIBLE STORYLINES
Experiences of gender dysphoria or exploring gender identity = part of my reality (communicating "how I am" but not "who I am").
I did not choose to experience gender dysphoria or gender-identity questions, but I honestly do not know the cause and may never know it.
Having gender dysphoria or gender-identity questions is a part of my experience, but it does not have to be central to my identity; there are many facets to who I am as a person.
I have a lot of areas of focus in my life, not just my experience of gender dysphoria or gender-identity questions.
Being transgender is part of my identity. However, I am a complex person, and I am more than anyone's definition of transgender or another gender identity.
I do not know how I came to experience gender dysphoria or gender-identity questions, but I can consider what these things mean to me today and the steps I take from here.

(Adapted with permission from Yarhouse, 2015, p. 135.)

Figure 9.2. Other possible storylines

Over time, clients can begin to sketch out a draft of their own story of their gender identity. This story is informed by the stories told about transgender persons by their religious faith community and by the mainstream LGBTQ+ community and broader culture. Clients can begin to pull together threads from any of the sources that have shaped their original beliefs and assumptions about gender identity, as well as new insights that they have today about the story they are currently writing (see worksheet 9.3).

Our clients can indeed write their own scripts for themselves and their journeys. Also, it is not uncommon for scripts and narratives to be edited over time. This is a normal part of the process, and as people learn and grow they can feel freedom to edit their scripts. Granted, some of their scripts may one day resemble someone else's primary script—but our clients will benefit from taking ownership over when, where, and how much this resemblance matters on their stage.

WORKSHEET 9.1. STORIES FROM DIFFERENT COMMUNITIES: RELIGIOUS FAITH COMMUNITY

Directions: What did you hear in your religious faith community growing up about people who experience a different gender identity or identify as transgender or gender nonbinary? Begin by listing words/phrases that you recall. Then write a summary statement that captures what was communicated to you about people who experience a different gender identity or identify as transgender or gender nonbinary.

Words/phrases:

_____

_____

_____

_____

_____

_____

Summary statement:

_____

_____

_____

_____

_____

_____

_____

_____

_____

_____

_____

_____

_____

_____

WORKSHEET 9.2. STORIES FROM DIFFERENT COMMUNITIES: MAINSTREAM LGBTQ+ COMMUNITY, ENTERTAINMENT, MEDIA

Directions: What have you heard from the LGBTQ+ community, entertainment, and media about people who experience a different gender identity or identify as transgender or gender nonbinary? Begin by listing words/phrases that you recall. Then write a summary statement that captures what was communicated to you about people who experience a different gender identity or identify as transgender or gender nonbinary.

Words/phrases:

_____

_____

_____

_____

_____

Summary statement:

_____

_____

_____

_____

_____

_____

_____

_____

_____

_____

_____

_____

_____

_____

WORKSHEET 9.3. THE BEGINNING OF YOUR NEW STORY (COUNTERNARRATIVE)

Directions: Reflect on the elements you identified within the stories told about transgender and gender-diverse persons by your religious faith community and by the mainstream LGBTQ+ community, media, and entertainment. As you think of writing your own story about gender identity, what (if anything) resonates with you from any of the sources that have shaped your original assumptions about gender identity? What new insights have you gained that might be part of a counternarrative to these stories?

_____

_____

_____

_____

_____

_____

_____

_____

_____

_____

_____

_____

_____

_____

_____

_____

_____

_____

_____

_____

10

CHAPTERS IN ONE'S LIFE

Kenzo, age twenty-seven, was born male and has lived as a man (or a boy) for his entire life. But he has struggled since childhood with his gender identity. When we invited him in counseling to divide his life so far into chapters, he was able to identify a few distinct chapters. His earliest chapter (which lasted from age two until seven or so) was a time of innocence he titled, "Just Me." He said, "I just didn't think much about gender or anything like what everyone talks about today. I was just me." He described his next chapter as a roadblock: "This was a time when I felt I bumped into things that were said or expectations for me that functioned as kind of a gender roadblock. . . . It was my parents who seemed to be saying that I should do things differently. Not play some of the games I played, like house, or not play with the toys I favored, like Barbies. Some of those toys or games were just gone. I'd ask about them, but they weren't there anymore. My parents were like, 'You outgrew your Barbies.' There was a lot there that was unspoken." Subsequent chapters ultimately led him to talk with someone in therapy about his gender identity and faith. Though he struggled to identify a chapter for the work we were doing in therapy, he felt this was the right time in his life to pursue therapy.

In our chapter on assessment, we discussed how clients can frame their experience of gender identity as a book with many chapters. In this chapter, we want to revisit this narrative strategy, giving special attention to how clients can be invited to reflect on the chapter they are currently writing in therapy and the chapters they hope to write in the coming years. Clients may not all have a clear idea of what they want from therapy. Some may want a place to discuss their gender identity and faith; others may want counsel on how to relate to their family or broader faith community. Some may bring in family members who they hope will be a source of support to them in their life's current and future chapters.

One of the keys to the narrative approach is to help clients understand who they consider the audience of their life's chapters to be. All of us have audiences to whom our stories are addressed. If a client's reflection on their life's chapters is to be maximally effective, they must take stock of who has been their audience for these chapters. What have been the frequent reactions of audience members as the story unfolds? Whose presence in the audience has been helpful? Whose responses have been hurtful and shaming? How can the client navigate audience members who continue to show up without invitation? Worksheets 10.1 and 10.2 can offer an opportunity to answer these questions.

PROCESSING NEGATIVE EXPERIENCES

As clinicians process this question of an audience with our clients, we will likely encounter stories of experiences that have negatively impacted them. Self-stigma is a reality for many members of minority groups, as we have already discussed, and it is certainly a common struggle for those exploring gender-identity questions. Since many clients do not understand what self-stigma is, this conversation about life's chapters can be a valuable opportunity for clinicians to provide education about the nature of self-stigma and the way it emerges in therapy for many people in an ongoing way. After all, the stories of peoples' lives can be immensely painful, and asking them to express their identity in a story is no simple task.

Especially when the chapters of a client's life involve traumatic experiences, we want to ensure that clients have adequate skills for processing such negative experiences before they begin to venture into them. A trauma-informed approach both cautions a client that the process of therapy may be dysregulating and paces that process in such a way that the client is not flooded. In fact, we have worked with individuals who never anticipated how painful it would be to look back on previous chapters of their life, and we have had to slow down the process of exploration in order to address emerging mood symptoms that were not a concern when we started therapy.

> *Chloe is a natal female who identifies as genderfluid and introduced themselves with they/them/their pronouns. They weren't quite sure if this identity fit them— gender-identity exploration was a new concept for them—but this was the identity they had landed on at the start of therapy. Chloe was invited to reflect*

on the chapters of their life leading up to the present. They explained that they didn't begin to experience gender-related distress until age ten or eleven. The chapter before their distress began in earnest was titled "Just Couldn't Fit In." Chloe's mom was hyperfeminine in all the ways Chloe was not: a "powerhouse attorney" who wore pencil skirts and high heels to almost every occasion. Chloe recalled that they had never been that way. In fact, they were quite comfortable if they never wore anything other than flat shoes, and they had stopped wearing makeup about five years ago. Throughout their school years, they went to a private school where they were expected to wear a skirt, and they hated every day of it. They often looked at their mom and thought, "What is wrong with me that I don't want to wear what she does?"

This sense of "not fitting in" was only heightened when they hit puberty— Chloe's second chapter—and their mom started to say things like, "How are you going to get a boyfriend if you never make yourself presentable?" Chloe's mom would critique Chloe for wearing "way too much black." Peers at school made things worse; Chloe shared numerous stories about peers taunting them for "basically being a boy" and assuring them that "we would like you more if you would just try a little harder to look good." Chloe titled this chapter "Basically a Boy." In their next chapter, they recalled focusing more on school and sports, settling into the reality that they would never be satisfied with being a girl. They titled this chapter "No Place to Go" because the ridicule kept coming, but they didn't have any sense of direction in responding to it.

Processing negative experiences allows clients like Chloe to make new meaning and ascribe different attributions to their experiences of discrimination rather than allowing these interactions to reinforce unhelpful beliefs about themselves, lead to chronic invalidation, and ultimately make it difficult to connect to and express painful affect (Sloan & Berke, 2018). We also want to help our clients reflect on how they would like to respond to the microaggressions or macroaggressions they encounter today, equipping them to anticipate and interact with people who make covertly or overtly offensive comments to them.

It is important to note that microaggressions and macroaggressions can go unnoticed for a variety of reasons. If a person has become used to negative reactions from others, they may have adapted to their circumstances by normalizing others' behavior. If a person's family of origin is a frequent source of negative and mocking comments about LGBTQ+ people, for example, it is important to further assess how, if, and when these comments were addressed by the client, and what the reactions of family members were when the comments were addressed. If your client has never addressed these comments, this may be an important opportunity to begin to challenge messaging that could be immensely damaging to their gender-identity exploration. Discussing such issues with your client will also provide space for you as the therapist to begin to model responding assertively to hostile comments, and to invite your client to notice how much they have become accustomed to hurtful experiences out of necessity.

There are certainly times when a client like Chloe may choose not to respond to microaggressions or verbal insults from others. While Chloe's decision not to respond may partially stem from internalized self-stigma, other factors may also be at play. It can be helpful for clients to understand how such interactions influence their mood, sense of safety in their environment, and beliefs about self and others. Clients may also want to think through, and even begin to make concrete plans for, how they will respond to microaggressions and insults once they feel ready to do so. Chloe might benefit, for instance, from deciding which settings and people most merit a response, especially those people with whom Chloe hopes to have an ongoing relationship.

PAST HURTS AND THE THERAPEUTIC ALLIANCE

The chapters that precede a client's current phase of life, both within and outside of therapy—including their past negative experiences—will inform the client's capacity to build a strong therapeutic alliance. Since our field understands the therapeutic alliance to be the best indicator of therapeutic gains, it is important for clinicians to pay close attention to the possible impact of past hurts on this alliance.

> Take, for instance, Kelly, a transgender female who presented to a first session with a cisgender female therapist. Kelly briefly commented that on the way into the office she saw a group of women staring at her. She spoke candidly about the judgment she could feel, saying, "Cis women just will never get me."

Rather than challenging such a comment directly, it has been helpful to name and honor the multitude of experiences that might inform such a thought. Kelly benefited from being able to elaborate on the challenging interactions that have informed her sense that cisgender women "always respond" to her with judgment. Another helpful question might be, "What are some of the things cis women do not get about you?"

In addition, the therapist working with Kelly may want to explore Kelly's fears, insecurities, hopes, and doubts as she enters into therapy with a cisgender female therapist. She can talk with Kelly about how important it is for Kelly to share the moments when she feels misunderstood by her therapist since these moments are inevitable in any therapeutic relationship. Kelly can consider the barriers she may feel about giving feedback to her therapist— who of course might symbolize a position of power, privilege, and even oppression to her—and strategize ways to overcome these barriers. The therapist will also benefit from sharing the attention she gives to fostering awareness of and addressing implicit biases that can affect this work (Cochran et al., 2018). This conversation can offer an important opportunity for Kelly not only to practice processing her past negative experiences but also to begin advocating for herself in ways that empower her and do not leave her helpless in moments of misunderstanding.

Just as it is important for clients to understand the barriers to their own assertiveness when they encounter microaggressions, clients should also reckon with the barriers that could keep them from asserting themselves in therapy. If Kelly experiences misunderstandings in therapy (as she inevitably will at times), she must be able to speak up in those moments. In order to foster the therapeutic alliance, it will be helpful to normalize the way you as the therapist will "miss" Kelly from time to time; invite Kelly to be open about those moments rather than internalizing them as a sign that she is to blame. The encouragement from the therapist to do so is often especially necessary in client-therapist relationships, where a power differential is evident. We will often ask a client, "What would it be like to tell me when I misunderstand you? What might get in the way of you telling me I've missed you? What could I do to help you feel more free to do so?"

TAKING BACK THE PEN

As clients explore the chapters of their lives, we invite them to remember that, regardless of the hurtful things they have been through, they are in the process of writing a new chapter. We begin to invite them at this stage to "take back the pen." That is, we recognize that others have weighed in on the scripts our clients have been reading from, especially those in earlier chapters of their life. By asking them to "take back the pen," we are inviting them to take ownership over the new chapter currently being created in their life.

One way of accessing this step is to have your client imagine they are on a stage. A person to their right walks toward them and hands them a script. Their eyes scan the first page, and they read: "My name is _____, and I experience gender dysphoria." You can ask them, "What would you like the rest of the script to say? What are you reading from your own script right now? Is there any part of your script that you would like to change in this next period of your life?"

KEY PEOPLE

We remind our clients that many key people have been part of the various phases of their lives up to this point. These same people may also claim ownership over the stages that our clients step out onto.

That is, a father might say, "If you don't read from the script I am holding in my hands for this chapter of your life, then you must get off my stage."

A mother might say, "All my life I looked forward to you reading from my script, and now you disappoint me so very much. How could you leave the stage I so carefully designed for you?"

A friend might say, "Why not accept the script that I read about on the internet, or the one I have been following in my own life? It really sounds a lot like you too."

A religious leader or faith community might say, "Here is the script from God—read it, act it out, or you can't be on our stage."

At this point, we offer a few more reflection questions that can be clinically useful:

- Who are the owners of the stage that you value?

- What are the scripts you believe these stage owners have given you to read?

- What would you gain by editing the script and making it your own, owning your own stage, and being or providing your own encouragement?

- What would you lose by writing your own script, owning your own stage, and being your own source of encouragement?

- Who are your audience members today? How can their perspective of you and your script be beneficial to you? How does their perspective challenge you?

- How can you identify and benefit from the wisdom, maturity, and discernment of people in your family and community? What strategies can you employ to keep the stage from being an all-or-nothing experience for you? Who do you need near you?

- Are there stages you willingly stand on and scripts you willingly read from because the owners of those stages and writers of those scripts are people you trust?

After reflecting on the key stakeholders and stage owners in clients' previous phases of life, we remind clients that we know people who have said, "I have determined that I will create my own stage. I will write my own script. I will learn to give myself my own applause and invite other key people to applaud as well. I will make peace with God on my own path." Alternatively, we know people who have said, "I have determined that I will stand on a stage owned by a God whom I trust. I will follow a script I have received from God. I will learn to listen to God as my audience and listen for God's applause." There are many, many possible responses to these prompts. Your role as a clinician is to explore these options with your clients as they navigate questions of gender identity and faith.

We emphasize to clients repeatedly that their decision about which script(s) they want to read from need not be "all-or-nothing" We invite clients to work with their family, community, and trusted mentors and peers to gain counsel, discernment, and input as they take on their next chapter. For a person to create their own stage has its risks, especially if that stage lacks input from a wise, mature, and discerning community.

We could also highlight for clients that when a person is onstage, they sometimes lose perspective. An audience certainly has a perspective our client may not be able to see while they are onstage. Thus, audience members are an important part of the story each person tells. Selecting the members of this audience is likewise important. This brings us to our next chapter, considering who will be there to support and encourage clients through the next chapters of their lives.

WORKSHEET 10.1. YOUR CHAPTER TODAY

Directions: If you think of your life as a book with many chapters, let's take a look at the chapter being written today. This includes your time in counseling. Take a few moments to answer the following questions.

How would you describe this chapter?

_____

_____

_____

_____

_____

_____

_____

_____

What title would you give it?

_____

Who are the key people who figure prominently in this chapter of your life and why?

_____

_____

_____

_____

_____

_____

_____

What are some of the themes that come up in this chapter?

_____

_____

_____

_____

_____

WORKSHEET 10.2. YOUR NEXT CHAPTER

Directions: If you think of your life as a book with many chapters, let's take a look at the chapter you want to write next, after your time in counseling is completed. Take a few moments to answer the following questions.

How would you describe that next chapter?

_____

_____

_____

_____

_____

_____

_____

_____

What title would you give it?

_____

Who are the key people who figure prominently in the next chapter of your life and why?

_____

_____

_____

_____

_____

_____

_____

_____

What are some of the themes that come up in this chapter?

_____

_____

_____

_____

_____

11

SOJOURNERS AND
TRAVELING COMPANIONS

SOCIAL SUPPORT IS A CRUCIAL AVENUE for connection, fostering resilience in the face of life's challenges. For those navigating gender identity who are also people of faith, however, their intersecting identities as both people of faith and gender minorities can complicate their search for social support.

This chapter addresses the importance of social support. The question for your client is, Who do you need near you as you embark on this next chapter? Experiencing gender dysphoria can be a lonely experience. Some people say that they feel they have always been different, that they have always felt like they were on the outside looking in. This description may or may not match your client's experience. In either case, we want to equip clients with strategies for effective self-disclosure, including how to identify safe people to disclose to, how to make the most of descriptive language, and how to time their disclosure effectively.

IDENTIFYING SOJOURNERS AND TRAVELING COMPANIONS

An important aspect of therapy, especially as a person begins to explore gender identity without a fixed outcome, is to identify sojourners and traveling companions who can journey alongside the person. These sojourners and traveling companions should be people who feel emotionally, physically, and spiritually safe to the person navigating gender identity and faith.

Said another way, therapy can be a place to determine whom clients can trust with their gender-identity journey. People do this work intuitively to some degree, identifying others who are able to receive and appreciate aspects of our experience. Part of this process is trial and error. Over time, our ability to identify safe people, and our belief that safe people exist, is impacted by others' responses to our past efforts at vulnerability.

Unfortunately, not everyone is safe, especially when it comes to sharing about gender identity. Great damage has been done when people have disclosed their questions or identities to unsafe confidants. We want to help our clients avoid these people, if possible, as such experiences can lead to internalized shame. We also do not want clients to foreclose on the possibility that they can identify safe people to share their journey with.

We often ask clients how they knew someone was a safe person to whom they could disclose any aspect of their experience. What common reactions told them someone was trustworthy? What signs indicated that a person was unsafe? What had past (or present) therapists done or said to show they were safe or unsafe? What postures had the client taken with others to communicate openness and ability to receive a vulnerable part of someone's journey?

We often frame the discussion with our clients in this way: one of the most common ways to identify safe people in relation to a particular experience is to listen to how someone talks about "people like you"—that is, people who share the same experience. Someone dealing with mental health concerns may want to pay close attention to how their friends and family members talk about people with mental health concerns before disclosing their own experience. A person considering coming out as gay or lesbian might listen carefully to how others talk about sexuality. Whenever a client discloses gender-identity concerns to us, then, we encourage them to think through how transgender people, or people navigating gender identity, are talked about by the people in their own life.

Many of the youth we have worked with too readily discount the possibility of sharing their story with parents or other authority figures. Their attitude is often shaped by YouTube videos of traumatic disclosures occurring in Christian homes. Without discounting the truth of these stories, we want youth to critically evaluate the likelihood of a similar reaction in their own home. Conversely, we have worked with youth who expected a positive response without good reason for this expectation, stepping into hurtful interactions with very little preparation. Worksheet 11.1 is useful in evaluating past experiences.

There are times when parents, pastors, youth ministers, children, and loved ones are unsafe. We want to help a client appreciate who might be unsafe and how they have come to know that this person is unsafe. Off-the-cuff comments that are shaming can be a cue that it is not the right time to open up to someone. However, the absence of these comments does not inherently make a person safe. Some loved ones may talk positively about transgender people broadly and yet respond unkindly to their own loved one's disclosure of gender-identity questions.

Regardless of how a client anticipates their loved ones will respond to disclosure about gender identity, it is important to plan for a variety of possible responses (see Yarhouse & Zaporozhets, in press). Worksheet 11.2 can be helpful in this assessment. Planning for best-case scenarios and worst-case scenarios will allow a client to feel more prepared to navigate disclosure. In cases where negative—or even violent—responses seem likely, we have found it helpful to engage in safety planning. This involves identifying a safe place to go following disclosure, notifying trusted people who can check in after the disclosure occurs, and making an exit plan in case the situation becomes dangerous. Thankfully, we have yet to work with someone who has had to utilize their safety plan in a worst-case scenario. In fact, disclosures to family members often go much better than expected. But much of the outcome of a disclosure is predicated on advance preparation, which often lays the foundation for a successful conversation. The fact that disclosure often goes better than expected can reassure those clients who might tend toward catastrophizing, without invalidating their real fears.

APPROACHING DISCLOSURE

Disclosure can be significant to some people's journey of gender-identity development. It can also be fraught with anxiety, experiences of rejection, and pain. We want to acknowledge that individuals differ widely in how open they wish to be about their gender-identity journey. Some are eager to disclose throughout therapy while others would rather be known in this way by only a few people. Some clients have been open about their gender identity for many years but face new challenges as they move to a new home, enter a new workplace, transition into college, or seek out a new faith community. Still others choose to wait to share their experience with anyone besides their therapist, perhaps because they are just now adjusting to naming that experience in therapy.

Disclosure can be especially difficult in the realm of gender-identity exploration because of the range of outcomes available to people wrestling with gender identity. As clinicians, we must take care not to impose on our clients a fixed outcome of what disclosure ought to look like. Instead, we should think critically with clients about what it looks like for them to be known by people in their life, without assuming that disclosure always ought to send a person along one particular path with regard to gender-identity consolidation. Worksheet 11.2 can help clients evaluate the possibilities.

As clients discern whether, how, and when to disclose their experience to others, it is important for them to think through the costs and benefits of disclosure and nondisclosure. With whom will it be particularly beneficial or costly to withhold this aspect of their experience, and to what extent? Opening the door to dialogue about one's journey with safe people has great value, but doing so with unsafe people can be enormously detrimental. Too often we consult with clients who have just endured very damaging disclosures. When such disclosures occur, the client's ability to process such experiences is paramount.

In cases where disclosure hasn't occurred yet, a good starting place in therapy is for clients to begin identifying safe people with whom they could potentially share about their gender identity (see worksheet 11.3). Even if a client is not planning on disclosing their gender-related distress any time soon, this exercise is still valuable. Helpful questions include: What qualities do I look for in a person to identify them as safe? What are good indicators that a person may not be safe to talk to? How does this person talk about other people with experiences similar to mine? What language could I use once I identify a person as safe? How might my language and the depth of what I share differ from person to person and situation to situation?

Young people today may be especially prone to black-and-white thinking about disclosure. We have met with clients who feel the need to disclose to every person they meet in great detail, regardless of the potential ramifications and painful reactions this could subject them to. We have found it helpful to process with such clients what information is necessary to share (if they are willing to receive feedback from others about this) and to help them articulate their experience of gender identity in a way that considers how generational differences could influence the responses they receive.

DESCRIPTIVE LANGUAGE AND DISCLOSURE

We have already mentioned that language matters when it comes to gender identity. Earlier we described the various ways a person could describe their gender-identity journey using a range of labels, both privately and publicly.

The ways people think about gender identity, labels, and emerging gender categories often reflect significant generational differences. Terms like *transgender* and *gender nonbinary* are typically heard and understood very differently by young people than they are by older generations. Thus, when you discuss disclosure with your clients, you may want to explore together the different meanings various labels can have for a variety of people. While it is important in disclosure for the person exploring gender identity to find and use language honest to their experience, they may want to strategically consider the age, perspective, and assumptions of the person to whom they are disclosing. This kind of thoughtfulness can help people avoid unnecessarily misunderstanding or speaking past each other.

We have found that with older generations, descriptive language that avoids labels tends to be much more accessible and less prone to misunderstanding. Whereas most young people are merely being descriptive when they use labels like *transgender*, other generations might interpret these terms as incomprehensible or as representative of philosophical or theological presuppositions, regardless of whether the client subscribes to such presuppositions.

Regardless of the language a person uses to describe their gender-identity journey, we encourage clients who choose to use a label in their disclosure to offer the meaning of that label in order to increase understanding of their experience and to reduce the likelihood of miscommunication. Clients may also find it helpful to share what drew them to a particular label rather than merely stating the label and hoping others will appreciate the value they find within it.

Young people in particular are sometimes prone to acting extremely confident about the label they use and their assuredness that this label fits. Their confidence is often an attempt to guard against the questions or negative reactions of others. However, especially in cases where gender-identity concerns seem to have emerged suddenly in later adolescence, this confidence often leads adults to want to challenge the narrative presented and play the devil's advocate. If such an interaction seems likely, we actually encourage young people to highlight their own thoughtful questioning of the labels they use. Likewise, they may want to express their curiosity about the way their gender-identity conflict does not seem to align with the historical course of gender dysphoria that is documented in the literature. By anticipating the concerns trusted adults in their lives may have and giving voice to these concerns, young people can demonstrate their maturity, balance, and thoughtfulness. Worksheet 11.4 can help a client prepare at least a preliminary script.

TIMING OF DISCLOSURE

Carl is a fifty-seven-year-old transgender person who has been wrestling with gender dysphoria for more than forty years. He currently publicly identifies as and is known as a man, but he privately identifies as a woman, which has put a strain on his marriage of twenty-nine years. He was in therapy for several years, and after about fourteen months of therapy he shared that he wanted to disclose his gender identity to his adult children. He reported feeling great shame in having kept this part of himself hidden. While he was unsure at this time whether he would pursue a full social transition, he did want his children to know that this experience was part of his life. He worked in therapy on drafting a letter he could share with his children when the time was right.

When approaching disclosure, it is also important to think about when to disclose. Timing can make a difference with how a disclosure is received by loved ones. It can also make a difference in how equipped a client feels to navigate the conversations that may follow disclosure. Given the increasing pressure we see, especially on young people, to be open about aspects of identity that may still be in process, we often encourage young people to weigh the value of their disclosures rather than feeling like they have to share their gender-identity exploration indiscriminately. We do not take the posture that everyone has a right to know a person's gender identity. Rather, we try to help clients appreciate that they can share this aspect of their identity in their own time, with the people they choose.

Some of our clients have benefited from considering whom they might need to disclose to, based on where they are in the process of gender-identity exploration. For example, some clients may be "out" to everyone in their social network, yet they still have not told those living in their home. We have seen this dynamic most often with youth or emerging adults. Such cases can present a variety of challenges, especially if the client has begun transitioning socially and is at risk of having their identity accidentally discovered by others before they disclose it. In these cases, clients who do not live near family may need to disclose prior to an approaching holiday, unless they would rather present in a different way during their next family gathering to reduce conflict.

Others may weigh their disclosures on a need-to-know basis, delaying disclosures that might be more challenging at times when their mental health is compromised. Still others find that, given how early they are in their journey of gender-identity exploration, they do not want to disclose to people who may foreclose on the meaning of such exploration.

For Carl, disclosure had already taken place with his wife. That disclosure was painful for both of them, but it also helped his wife make sense of some of the behavior she knew had been taking place throughout their twenty-nine years of marriage: Carl's use of makeup from time to time, some cross-dressing behavior he attempted to keep hidden, and so on. Carl had also disclosed to a select group of people, including other transgender and gay individuals at a local LGBTQ+ support group that met monthly. But disclosure to his adult children was another topic altogether. What was prompting his desire to share this part of himself? What did it mean? How would they respond? What did his wife think of this decision? What would their children think of her and of their marriage? These were some of the questions Carl wrestled with as he crafted his letter and worked through the different layers of meaning, motivations, and possible consequences.

IDENTIFYING ADDITIONAL AVENUES FOR SUPPORT

Jay is a sixty-four-year-old transgender male who came to see us in the middle of a divorce. He was in the process of seeking out a new faith community. After his recent social transition and use of hormone therapy, he was no longer allowed to serve in his former church's choir, and he had experienced a range of difficult interactions with his faith community. He was experiencing greater loneliness since his transition than he had ever encountered previously, sparking a new bout of his long-standing depression. Navigating his adjustment to a full social transition and presentation as male was complex in itself, but Jay was also finding that he longed for community now more than ever; and yet his primary source of community—his faith community—was no longer able to support him.

Especially for transgender people of faith who come to therapy in the midst of an experience like Jay's, connecting to social support and resources is complicated but essential. Making these connections requires awareness of and willingness to research the distinct resources available to Jay and others, both those from the local LGBTQ+ community (e.g., an LGBTQ+ center) and those from local faith communities.

Jay initially struggled to connect with his local LGBTQ+ center since his values as a person of faith contrasted with the values of many of the people he met there. Jay, a socially conservative person and an older adult, felt disconnected and isolated when he visited the center; many people there were young adults and were hostile toward the faith he had grown up in and still loved. Still, even though much of what the center offered was not a good fit for him, it did connect him to resources related to aspects of his experience that he could not find elsewhere.

The kinds of resources a client needs may vary widely. We have worked with clients who are struggling as a result of recent or pending threats of homelessness. Others have come to us with difficulties navigating workplace dynamics, or wrestling with workplace safety as they begin the process of social transition. In therapy, clinicians can help a client think through potential challenges and feel more capable of navigating them. In work settings, and especially in faith-based settings, it is invaluable to know what resources and people a client can turn to if they are struggling with discrimination or harmful responses. As we've discussed previously, there will be room here to help your client practice assertiveness and develop strategies for coping with challenging environments.

As clients invite others to accompany them on their gender-identity journey, we hold in mind that much of our work in therapy with these clients involves the same sorts of support we would offer to any person we meet with. As clinicians develop skills to work with diverse groups, including those navigating gender identity, it is essential to remember that many pieces of therapy apply across the board. We turn now to the essential work of helping clients unpack their feelings, both around gender identity and about their lives as a whole.

WORKSHEET 11.1. PROCESSING HARMFUL MESSAGES/RELATIONSHIPS

Directions: It's important to consider the harmful and damaging responses that have come up when you shared about gender-identity questions. Take a few moments to answer the following questions.

What damaging reactions and messages have I heard from others regarding my gender-identity questions/process?

_____

_____

_____

_____

_____

What responses have been directed toward me or about me that have left me confused and/or hurt?

_____

_____

_____

_____

_____

For the individuals who have responded poorly to me, what do I wish they would have said and done differently?

_____

_____

_____

_____

_____

To what degree have I responded in unhealthy/harmful ways to these messages from others? To what degree have I responded in healthy/adaptive ways?

_____

_____

_____

_____

_____

WORKSHEET 11.2. WEIGHING DISCLOSURE

Directions: Sharing about your experience is never easy. In fact, it is likely to make you feel anxious if you choose to share with someone that you are exploring gender identity and/or experiencing gender dysphoria. You may be unsure whether it is worth it to open up about this. Let's start by considering the following questions.

What would be the pros or benefits of sharing my experiences with someone I trust?

_____

_____

_____

_____

_____

_____

_____

_____

_____

_____

_____

What would be the cons or risks of sharing my experiences with someone I trust?

_____

_____

_____

_____

_____

_____

_____

_____

_____

_____

What would it be like to keep everything about my experiences to myself? What has it been like so far? What will it be like ten to twenty years from now?

_____

_____

_____

_____

_____

_____

_____

What questions could I anticipate insofar as I choose to disclose? What questions do I feel confident answering, and what questions would be more difficult to answer?

_____

_____

_____

_____

_____

_____

_____

How healthy are my relationships overall? Are there any relationships that need to become healthier before I share about this experience? If so, which ones?

_____

_____

_____

_____

_____

_____

_____

WORKSHEET 11.3. IDENTIFYING SAFE PEOPLE

Directions: It's important to ask whom you can trust with the questions or concerns that have come up for you regarding your gender identity. Take a few moments to answer the following questions.

With whom might I feel comfortable sharing about my experiences of gender identity?

_____

_____

_____

_____

_____

_____

_____

What are some things or characteristics that make these people safe for me to share with?

_____

_____

_____

_____

_____

_____

_____

With whom might I not feel comfortable sharing my experiences of gender dysphoria?

_____

_____

_____

_____

_____

_____

_____

What are some things or characteristics that make these people unsafe for me to share with?

_____

_____

_____

_____

_____

_____

_____

_____

What are some of the ways that safe people can support me moving forward? What do I need from supports (space, further conversations, etc.)?

_____

_____

_____

_____

_____

_____

_____

_____

WORKSHEET 11.4. SHARING WITH SAFE PEOPLE

Directions: Take a few moments to answer the following questions.

What exactly would I like to tell the safe people in my life when it comes to my experience of gender dysphoria / gender identity?

_____

_____

_____

_____

_____

_____

_____

_____

_____

_____

_____

When exactly would I like to tell the safe people in my life about my experience of gender dysphoria / gender identity?

_____

_____

_____

_____

_____

_____

_____

_____

_____

_____

_____

_____

12

UNPACKING FEELINGS

Christy, a sixteen-year-old natal female, came to therapy at the urging of her parents. She had struggled with panic attacks for the past year. She had also disclosed feeling "like I am not a girl, at my core." Her parents, evangelical Christians, were unsure how to approach their child's statement and sought support. Christy had never been to therapy and was not too keen on being there. Her parents, feeling desperate to "figure out the gender piece," struggled to see the value of first addressing Christy's panic symptoms in therapy. In fact, when we explained that we wanted to prioritize these symptoms, which were impairing Christy's capacity to stay in school and perform academically, the parents put their foot down. They said they wanted us to prioritize gender-identity exploration because that was their chief difficulty. Christy supported her parents' preference, thinking that her panic symptoms were a result of her wrestling with gender identity. She often said, "I don't want to feel any emotions, and I don't like them." We shared our concern with this approach but temporarily honored the family's request. A month later, Christy and her parents changed their minds. The panic symptoms were getting worse, not better. Christy found that she was not able to explore gender identity deeply without first becoming more aware of her emotions. We shifted our approach to prioritize treating the panic attacks. Very soon, Christy had enough coping skills in place to manage her mood and was ready to return to processing gender identity.

An important message to communicate as a therapist is that no matter what pathway a person takes with regard to gender identity, there is value in becoming an expert on one's emotional experiences. Of course, a range of strategies is available for helping clients become more self-aware and emotionally intelligent. We are not necessarily offering something different from the available treatments; rather, we simply want to augment what you already know about helping people explore their emotions.

REMEMBERING FOUNDATIONAL THERAPEUTIC GOALS

In supervision and training we have seen clinicians become fixated on the work around gender identity. In the process, these clinicians can lose sight of the value of traditional therapeutic techniques to increase emotional insight and bring about greater capacity to manage difficult emotions.

We have consulted with therapists who are anxious about their work at the intersection of gender identity and faith. In part, it is out of these consultations that this book exists. We always encourage therapists to seek additional supervision, consultation, and training in order to establish competence in the area of gender identity. This is a vulnerable aspect of people's lives, and clinicians are expected to learn what we can in order to provide ethical care. At the same time, we have also found that when therapists are supporting a person exploring gender identity, they are prone to forget about the important foundational therapeutic goals applicable to all kinds of clients.

Take, for instance, Jen, a therapist who consulted with us about her work with a teen and their parents. The teen was seeking medical interventions through hormonal treatment and was open to therapy in supporting that process. Jen was very concerned with what she did and didn't know when it came to the interventions the client was pursuing and how to navigate the family dynamics therein. This was a worthwhile focus, and one we spent a great deal of time on. Still, we found it important to emphasize for Jen that she already possessed therapeutic skills that were important to bring into her work with the client.

We reminded Jen that, in the midst of all the focus on gender, it could be easy to forget that her client was a teenager and could benefit from learning how to manage and understand their emotions. Some teenagers we have worked with expect the work of therapy to address only the gender-identity interventions they are seeking. Yet therapy involves much more than just direct consideration of gender identity; traditional therapy techniques, rather than creating a barrier to gender exploration, can provide the necessary scaffolding for clients to gain insight into their emotions and develop distress-tolerance and emotional-regulation skills. These outcomes, we reminded Jen, will serve her client throughout their life, regardless of how they ultimately choose to consolidate their gender identity.

Insofar as a person has not done much therapy, the work of exploring feelings is an especially important initial goal of clinical work. Equipping a client with the capacity to become an expert on their emotional life will put them in a much better position to navigate a range of challenges as they move forward. Developing emotional awareness will also help them discern what their feelings around gender identity are working to communicate to them.

UNPACKING SHAME

When people experience paralyzing feelings, a common reaction is to give in to those feelings and give up. A client might experience self-pity, isolation, and abandonment: the sense that there is no one to help them through this experience. Our aim here is to offer a range of tools for managing painful feelings.

Shame is a powerful emotional experience that differs from guilt in important ways. Guilt is what people feel when they have the sense that "the thing I did was bad" whereas shame is what people feel when they have the sense that "I am bad."

When a person feels shame, it can often lead to enormous self-rejection. It leads clients to hold others at arm's length, expecting that they will be rejected. This dynamic makes the important work of building up supports nearly impossible if the work of reducing shame is not prioritized.

Even though ignoring painful feelings such as shame may seem easier to clients, denying the reality of these feelings can create enormous problems, especially when it comes to exploring gender identity. We have found that many people who deny or suppress their feelings will struggle with mental health concerns that make it difficult to explore and cope with gender dysphoria.

Ignoring feelings such as shame can certainly help your client temporarily avoid anxiety, but it can ultimately lead to these feelings manifesting in less helpful ways.

Jeff was a forty-year-old natal male who came to therapy wanting to explore gender identity. On a cognitive level he knew that he struggled with shame about his long-standing gender dysphoria. But he was sure that talking about the shame and other difficult emotions was "unnecessary" because it wouldn't help to talk about negative things. He wanted to figure out where to go from here, not harp on the past. He struggled to see the value in unpacking and learning to manage feelings of shame.

At the same time, as therapy progressed and as Jeff began to explore the chapters of his life, the painful memories came flooding in. He recalled shaming responses from childhood when he had secretly worn his sister's underwear and bras. He quickly realized he was not equipped to name, or to begin to manage, the feelings of shame inside him. His depression peaked, and the process of gender-identity exploration began to feel impossible.

When it came to looking for others to share his struggles with, Jeff would have no part in it. He was convinced that if other people knew this part of his story, they would reject him.

Over time, Jeff came to see that he was already doing a sufficient job at self-rejection, regardless of whether he ever let anyone else into his experience. He also came to see that talking about the sources of shame in his story, and beginning to challenge the core beliefs that flowed from this shame, allowed him to courageously open up to safe people about his shame, his other painful emotions, and even his gender dysphoria.

We as clinicians can educate our clients about how important adaptive coping is when dealing with difficult human emotions such as guilt and shame. Clients like Jeff can't always recognize the way shame keeps them stuck in old patterns of relating to themselves, serving as an enormous barrier to self-acceptance and growth. Jeff began to see that exploring his own shame and managing it when it reared its head would be a foundational skill in his work on exploring and sharing his experience of gender dysphoria with others.

Insofar as Jeff and other clients find themselves suppressing feelings like shame, we want to honor the fears that may be contributing to this suppression. What do they expect will happen if they let in a feeling like shame? Jeff feared it would "swallow" him, making him unable to see himself or others clearly. He was learning, though, that shame was already swallowing him in a different way, even while he worked so hard to ignore it.

INTERVIEWING FEELINGS

Another technique we have drawn from is the use of externalization techniques to approach difficult emotions. We want to assist a client in stepping outside of themselves when they are overwhelmed by difficult feelings, including fear, anxiety, and anger as well as gender dysphoria itself.

There is no shortage of ways to externalize an emotion and gain perspective of it. We have used the empty-chair technique in cases where a client wants to "interview" their emotions. For this technique, we invite the client to develop interview questions they could ask of their emotions; they then imagine their emotions sitting in a chair, ask questions of them, and hear their response.[1] Clients and clinicians also can work together to develop a range of interview questions specifically addressing gender dysphoria.

The empty-chair interview technique is meant to help a client confront the distressing emotions they are experiencing, interviewing those emotions as if they were a person. This technique can certainly feel odd for some people, but it can also help reduce fear, stress, and anxiety.

In the interview technique, pointed questions like these can help guide the time:

- Why have you come to visit me today?

- If I were to completely follow your emotional advice, where would that lead us both?

- Don't you think it is a bit unfair that you are trying to emotionally overwhelm me and win this argument?

- Do you think that other emotions should be allowed to speak their mind? What about reason? Shouldn't my thoughts and reason be allowed to weigh in as well? I thought we were a team?

This version of the interview technique lets a client "de-power" emotions and gain back a sense of control, especially when confronting emotions like shame that often make a person feel powerless.

RADICAL ACCEPTANCE OF GENDER DYSPHORIA

Distress around gender identity can be incredibly painful. Most of the people we work with share about moments in their life when they tried to run from this experience, deny it, overcompensate for it, or minimize its relevance. For these clients, radical acceptance becomes a relevant skill to help them acknowledge the reality of their experiences.

---

[1] Art forms provide another way to externalize feelings and hear what they are trying to communicate.

If someone does not want to accept the reality of their experience with gender dysphoria or gender-identity questions, there are several options available to them.

One person may try to change how they feel. This attempt can take the form of leaning into rigid gender stereotypes, in hopes that doing so will alleviate their discomfort. We don't recommend this approach, which often leads people to deny how they really feel about their gender dysphoria and can even increase their distress.

Another person may try to change their situation—but if the situation is not changeable, this is a wasted effort. For example, a young person may be unable or unready to consider changing their physical body to manage gender dysphoria, while some individuals hold personal or religious values that preclude them from pursuing these changes.

A third person could choose to deny that their circumstance is real, giving way to misery. This option is also not appealing or sustainable because there aren't very many people who sign up for a life of misery.

This is where radical acceptance comes in. Radical acceptance is not the same thing as giving up on making life more manageable. It is also not committing to a particular pathway to resolve gender identity. Rather, radical acceptance means acknowledging feelings and experiences as part of one's life at this moment. A person who responds to their gender dysphoria with radical acceptance acknowledges that this is an experience they are currently working through and working with.

There is hope in radical acceptance. Transformation can only begin when people acknowledge the existence of the thing they want to transform. Radical acceptance pushes back on the defensive posture of denial. Once a client can acknowledge that they deal with gender dysphoria, they can move forward in discerning what it means to transform this experience into a more manageable one.

EXPLORING FEELINGS AROUND GENDER DYSPHORIA

In addition to understanding a person's feelings about their life, their relationships, and their personhood, it is important to help a person understand their felt experience of gender dysphoria so that they can express it to others (see worksheet 12.1).

We will often ask a client about the degree to which they keep their gender dysphoria "locked away." We want to appreciate how this approach has functioned for them but also how it has limited their capacity to understand and share their experience of gender dysphoria with others.

Below is a series of helpful questions that can illuminate the reflexive ways people experience difficulties around their gender identity. Clients may want to respond to these questions in journal form in order to explore their emotional responses to their own gender incongruence:

- How do you feel about other people who experience gender dysphoria?
- How do you feel about yourself as you experience gender dysphoria?
- What concerns/apprehensions do you have about your own experience of gender dysphoria?
- Is there anything that discourages you about this experience?
- What motivates, encourages, or excites you about this experience?

It is striking to see how people's emotional responses to their own gender incongruence often vary greatly from the ways they respond to others with similar experiences. For example, many people are highly critical of their own gender incongruence while expressing sympathy and compassion for others in the same situation. This disparity between people's responses to themselves and their responses to others can shed light on the self-stigma often experienced by those navigating gender identity. Clinicians can help their clients challenge the differing standards and emotional responses they have toward their own experiences versus that of others.

Yet another valuable exercise has been asking a person to draw their gender dysphoria. The pain of dysphoria is palpable and excruciating at times for those who experience it, yet it can be difficult for others to imagine. This makes it difficult for people struggling with dysphoria to reach out for support since their struggle seems like a foreign emotional experience. Using an art form like drawing can help a client communicate their felt experience even when that experience is hard to access with words alone.

When we have asked clients to draw or speak about what their gender dysphoria feels like, we have gotten a range of responses. Sometimes it is helpful to share a few of these previous responses with a client, to help anchor them into possible ways of expressing their experience to others.

One client depicted dysphoria as a stomachache, one that they had all the time and that was draining their energy, and they were so tired of always having this ache.

Another client described dysphoria as dissonance in music that does not resolve.

Still another client likened dysphoria to working on a jigsaw puzzle, attempting to put together two pieces that "just don't fit." The client described looking around them in confusion, asking how it is that these pieces seemed to fit together for others.

It has been powerful to see how exploring the experience of gender incongruity through art, journaling, or other creative means can open up ways for a client to share their experience with loved ones and friends.

MANAGING DIFFICULT EMOTIONS

Teaching clients to understand their feelings is important because it allows them to begin figuring out how to manage those feelings effectively. As we conclude this chapter, we want to name and call attention to this dynamic so that the purpose of the chapter remains absolutely clear. Our hope is not that clients will become consumed with emotions without a path for alleviating their intensity. Rather, our hope is that clients will learn to reckon with their emotions and address them in healthy ways.

Here are some final reflection questions that can be useful in this regard:

- When you are overwhelmed with your gender dysphoria or other emotions such as fear, anxiety, or anger, what are some things you can do to step outside of yourself?

- When your gender dysphoria is distressing, what can you do to soothe yourself?

- Who can you talk to about your gender dysphoria? When? How often?

We turn now to another reason these skills are so important: they can help clients begin to put words to the way their faith and emotional experience of God factors into their gender-identity journey.

WORKSHEET 12.1. UNPACKING FEELINGS AROUND GENDER IDENTITY

Directions: Take some time to journal your response to several of the questions below.

1. Do you keep your questions or concerns about gender identity "boxed up"? If so, what would it be like to unpack your questions/concerns/experiences so that you can take a look at them?

_____

_____

_____

_____

_____

_____

2. What emotions come to mind when you think about your gender-identity concerns? If you have been trying to shut down your feelings, is there anything you might be afraid of?

_____

_____

_____

_____

_____

_____

_____

3. Many people have mixed feelings about having gender-identity questions or experiencing gender dysphoria. What about you? What is your particular mix of feelings?

_____

_____

_____

_____

_____

_____

4. Do you have a preferred gender identity? How would you describe that gender identity?

_____

_____

_____

_____

_____

_____

5. What are the feelings (and/or sensations) you usually get when you think of yourself as a man?

_____

_____

_____

_____

_____

_____

6. What are the feelings (and/or sensations) you usually get when you think of yourself as a woman?

_____

_____

_____

_____

_____

_____

7. What are the feelings (and/or sensations) you usually get when you think of yourself as another gender identity?

_____

_____

_____

_____

_____

_____

8. What are the feelings (and/or sensations) you usually get when you think of yourself as masculine?

_____

_____

_____

_____

_____

_____

9. What are the feelings (and/or sensations) you usually get when you think of yourself as feminine?

_____

_____

_____

_____

_____

10. What themes emerge and what observations can you make based on your answers to the questions above?

_____

_____

_____

_____

_____

_____

13

WHERE IS GOD?

A COMMON CONCERN among people we have worked with who are navigating gender identity and faith is their relationship with God. Many have been made to feel that their gender-identity questions preclude a relationship with God. Although people's local faith communities, pastors, mentors, parents, and peers are often their primary sources of support in navigating questions of faith, therapy can be a helpful adjunct in this exploration. We have also found that therapy can be a space where clients consider how their mental health concerns have impacted and been impacted by their relationship with God. This chapter will attend to these considerations.

There are many ways of understanding the relationship between faith and mental health, and many differing perspectives about the degree to which faith can help or harm individuals navigating gender identity. We know that many of our clients identify as people of faith and care deeply about the intersection of their faith and their gender-identity journey. We want to support them in their desire to turn toward God and faith, helping them look to God as a resource rather than being made to feel as if their only path forward is a life apart from God. Their intentional search regarding gender identity includes their faith, and it matters to them to be able to bring this faith into the therapeutic relationship.

Clinicians have many general assessment options for approaching faith and spirituality in therapy. We have already provided some questions that can be helpful in assessing the messaging around gender identity in a client's faith community. In this chapter, we want to focus on clients' personal faith and the way gender identity has impacted that faith.

We like to ask people a range of questions as we begin seeking to understand their personal faith and its relationship to gender identity. Many of our clients, especially those who have been exploring and wrestling with gender identity from a young age, have brought their questions to God in prayer. If they have not felt able to bring their questions to God, they have at least used prayer as a way to ask God to take away their gender-related distress. We have found it useful to normalize our clients' experiences by telling them how many gender minorities have feared that they cannot approach God unless their conflict is first resolved, as if merely experiencing such conflict means they are in a state of sin.

A good place to start is to unpack how much a client's personal relationship with God has focused on or includes questions around gender identity. If gender identity has not been a significant part of their relationship with God, we have found it helpful to understand why not. We might ask a client, How did you come to sense that such wrestling was not to be shared with God in prayer? What did you fear would happen if you did bring these things to God? What did happen insofar as you attempted to bring these things to God? How did other people model the intersection of gender identity and faith?

For some clients, particular spiritual disciplines or spiritual resources have helped them encounter God even while they have mixed feelings about how he sees them. Scripture reading, devotionals, spiritual and faith-based podcasts and webinars, the writings and testimonies of other Christians, active participation in a faith community, missions work, worship, and contemplative prayer have been particularly valuable to our clients. These disciplines become especially crucial when a client's faith community feels tenuous, whether because that faith community is struggling to accompany the client or because the community seems poised to reject them.

Consider Jake, a natal male in his late twenties who was struggling with gender dysphoria. He was not able to worship in public due to his insecurities about being perceived as male by others, but he had a great love for music as a means of worship. He felt that he couldn't encounter God through public worship until he had his gender identity all figured out. In therapy he came to appreciate that he could return to this spiritual discipline by playing music in the comfort of his home, leading close friends in worship in this way. He didn't need to feel like his connection with God hinged on his willingness to lead a church's worship in a more formal way at this time in his life.

Other individuals, like Peg, have shared about how certain spiritual disciplines have felt "off limits" to them. For Peg, personal prayer and private devotions seemed fruitless, devolving into cycles of rumination and shame around her gender-identity conflicts. Peg turned instead to corporate worship (or worship of God with a gathered community of others), active participation in a faith community, and missions work, finding that she could still access God through these disciplines when she found personal devotions to be much more difficult.

It is important to explore what pathways for connection with God are available to any given client. We recommend revisiting this question throughout a client's gender-identity exploration since their decisions around gender identity could influence their sense of connection to God and to a faith community.

SPIRITUALITY AS A MEANING-MAKING STRUCTURE

We have written elsewhere about the spiritual resources available to people navigating gender identity. Here we want to acknowledge the way spirituality can offer a meaning-making structure amid the difficulties clients face.

Many clients, we have found, feel guilt and shame for not already knowing the meaning in their suffering. They may struggle with anger at God for the way he has felt absent. The powerlessness some clients feel about their gendered experience can overwhelm them in much the same way grief does. They may feel as if a loving God would not subject his followers to the enduring pain they feel. These are important and valuable questions for clients to address within their faith community. Since some clients face challenges in connecting to their faith communities and sharing honestly about the nuances of their gender-identity conflicts, however, we have also seen value in making space for clients to process this grief in therapy. The problem of pain and suffering is one that many clients will wrestle with, but we have seen this wrestling to be particularly valuable for people of faith.

Normalizing the process of grief—which involves anger, sadness, fear, and a range of other emotions—is essential for inviting a client to begin to seek meaning in their particular pain. We have met with clients who fear that making a lament to God is itself sinful. We often remind those who wrestle with how to pray that one third of the psalms in Scripture are psalms of lament. If the psalms teach us how to pray, we tell our clients, it seems that an aspect of that prayer involves sharing our grief with God and lamenting.

As clients feel more able to bring their wrestling to God, we have witnessed them begin to ask God about their particular experience and seek to understand his plan in the midst of their pain. Some clients have found it helpful to look at how other Christians imbued their pain with moral value, seeing it as a pathway to sanctification rather than a punishment from God. They have sought out the writings of men and women of God who grapple with the question of suffering. Some of our clients have shared with us that their pain has made them more able to weather the storms of life alongside someone else who is struggling. Others have shared that they are more able to appreciate and endure suffering in community and model vulnerability in a way that enriches church life. Still others have found great meaning in uniting their own suffering to that of Christ.

> *Kari is a lesbian, Christian natal female who experiences gender dysphoria. She told us that uniting her suffering to Christ has helped her manage her gender dysphoria in a way that honors her personal values, without resorting to invasive interventions. She explained, "I was in prayer one evening and was reflecting on Jesus' incarnation in a human body. He took on this body that was limited and could not possibly reflect his personhood fully. He felt the limits of the body, which means I am not alone in my own sense of the limits of my body." This realization gave consolation to Kari in her journey, offering timely support when she wrestled with feeling like she was flawed in some irrevocable way because of her gender dysphoria.*

Clients may find it helpful to journal about the ways God has used their dysphoria or other ongoing and enduring difficulties (see worksheet 13.1) to foster spiritual maturity or to equip them to help others in some way. Questions like these can serve as prompts:

- How has God been present to you through your enduring challenges, including gender-related questions?

- How has God used your experiences to provide insights into the world around you or to make the world around you a better place?

- What qualities and aspects of your character has God been forming through this experience?

REDUCING SHAME

Therapists working in this realm should keep in mind the important concept of spiritual abuse: namely, the way religious ministers or spiritual authority figures can misuse their power to control a person's spiritual walk in a way that does harm (Ward, 2011). For those navigating gender identity, spiritual abuse poses yet another barrier to encountering God and discovering his presence in their gender-identity journey. Experiences of abuse may make it difficult for clients to engage in spiritual disciplines; part of the work of therapy may be to reduce shame around this struggle since these disciplines are often foundational to the spiritual lives of people of faith. Sadly, many clients will blame themselves for experiencing barriers in connecting to their faith. They may fail to appreciate the impact of hurtful messaging, the abuse of important mentors, or any number of other adverse factors on their hesitancy to approach God in prayer and the shame they feel about this hesitancy.

It is important to note that reducing shame is a challenging and long-term component of the work most clients will do in therapy around their spirituality and gender identity. In the last chapter, we discussed strategies for unpacking and processing emotions like shame. There is no one intervention that can single-handedly alleviate years of shame. However, a number of interventions can help shed light on and attenuate shame.

A range of interventions called "God-image work" can help clients understand the way their relationship with God may be impaired by shame (Moriarty & Hoffman, 2014). These interventions can also help clients identify the important people who played a role in modeling their current understanding of God. Thinking carefully about these factors of their spiritual life can reduce their self-blame for the distance they perceive in their relationship with God; it can also allow them to take ownership over ways they want to begin moving toward a deeper relationship with God.

> For example, a sixteen-year-old natal female, Amy, came for a consultation with her parents. They were from the "Deep South," Amy shared, "where there is no place for me." Amy had been struggling with gender-identity concerns since she was four or five years old, but the last year had been particularly difficult. At one point in our work together, we shared with Amy's mother that Amy did not choose to experience gender dysphoria; it was not an act of "willful disobedience" on her part. Amy's mother burst into tears. Through her sobbing she found the

words she was searching for: "*Every pastor we went to—and we went to three before we came here—every pastor said it was 'willful disobedience' on Amy's part. We didn't know what to think. We didn't know whether to discipline Amy, which is what we would do if it was disobedience. At least that's how we have handled anything else as parents. When a kid lies, you discipline. When a kid steals, you discipline. So, we didn't know what to make of our own pastors' advice.*"

Sometimes reducing shame means challenging claims that have been contributing to shame. When a person is told that what they are doing (in this case, experiencing gender dysphoria) is an act of willful disobedience against God, this accusation will almost certainly lead to shame. Does Amy have choices to make? Of course; everyone does. But to say that Amy chose to experience gender dysphoria is a dangerous claim based on limited pastoral experience with people navigating gender-identity questions.

PSALM OF LAMENT

Psalms of lament have been used by Christians, even within sacred texts, to express fears and concerns to God. Clients may find it powerful to apply the empty-chair technique to their relationship with God, addressing their own lament to God in the midst of painful experiences (see worksheets 13.2 and 13.3). This is an integrative technique that sensitively draws from the faith tradition of a client, when such a tradition is present. Clinical research indicates that integrative interventions can be just as effective as interventions that do not integrate elements of a client's religion/spirituality (Hook et al., 2010; Smith et al., 2007).

We want to emphasize that an integrative approach like this one does not fit the longing or therapeutic process of every client. It is best used when a client wants to approach God with their questions, doubts, and longings but fears doing so because they were raised in a faith environment that shamed them for their questions. In fact, when we have used this approach, we have found it helpful to introduce the concept without making use of it immediately, leaving space for the client to revisit it at a later time or weigh their level of comfort with it.

We close this chapter by recognizing that its content is particularly relevant to those actively wrestling with the integration of their faith and gender identity. Some clients, for a variety of reasons, may not connect with the interventions herein, or may feel more comfortable exploring faith and spirituality with relevant guides in their faith community. Sadly, we find that many clients look to therapists for support in this work of integration because they have already tried turning to faith communities and have not found guides willing to enter into these questions with them. Ideally, faith communities would provide space for gender-diverse people to wrestle with their spiritual questions. Regardless, we certainly want therapy to attend to these questions, especially when they go unanswered in other contexts.

WORKSHEET 13.1. EXPLORING GOD AND ENDURING CHALLENGES

Directions: Take a few minutes to reflect on the following questions and journal your response. The questions have to do with the ways God has used enduring difficulties to foster spiritual maturity and equip you to help others in some way.

What are the ways God has been present to you through your enduring challenges, including gender-related questions?

_____

_____

_____

_____

_____

_____

_____

How has God used your experiences to provide insights into the world around you or to make the world around you a better place?

_____

_____

_____

_____

_____

_____

_____

What qualities and aspects of your character has God been forming through this experience?

_____

_____

_____

_____

_____

_____

WORKSHEET 13.2. A PSALM OF LAMENT

Directions: Read through several of the psalms of communal lament, such as Psalm 44, 60, 74, 79, 80, 85, or 90. Spend some time reflecting on the idea of lament: the deeply felt expression of sorrow, pain, grief, questions, doubts, and longings. In the space that follows, consider writing your own psalm of lament in which you share with God the questions and feelings you have.

_____

_____

_____

_____

_____

_____

_____

_____

_____

1. What questions, fears, or doubts did you note in your psalm?

_____

_____

_____

_____

2. What emotions can you identify in your psalm?

_____

_____

_____

_____

3. Who can you discuss your feelings/questions/doubts with?

_____

_____

_____

_____

WORKSHEET 13.3. MY FAITH PROCESS

Directions: Take a few minutes to reflect on the following questions and journal your response. The questions have to do with your experience of God in relation to your exploration of gender.

1. **What questions do you want to ask God about your gender identity?**

   _____

   _____

   _____

   _____

   _____

2. **What feelings do you have about God when you think about your experiences of gender identity?**

   _____

   _____

   _____

   _____

   _____

3. **What feelings do you have about God when not thinking about your experiences of gender identity?**

   _____

   _____

   _____

   _____

   _____

4. **How do you think God feels toward you?**

   _____

   _____

   _____

   _____

   _____

14

COPING AND
MANAGEMENT STRATEGIES

Candace is a thirty-eight-year-old transgender woman. She was born male and struggled with gender dysphoria from as early as she can remember. She recalls being more effeminate than the other boys growing up, which caused her parents a lot of concern. In that era her parents thought she was likely gay; they did not know what it could mean to experience a different gender identity. When Candace told them about her gender identity during college, it led to a lot of confusion, conflict, and misunderstanding. Candace has often felt she is alone in her gender-identity journey. She has made a social transition that she describes as "critical" to her well-being. More recently, she has begun using hormone therapy to feminize her appearance but has not elected to pursue gender-confirmation (sex-reassignment) surgery.

Morgan is a forty-one-year-old natal female who identifies as a woman and has been married for fifteen years to her husband. They have two children together. When Morgan came to see us, she shared that she has suffered from gender in-congruence for many years. She manages her dysphoria by keeping her hair short and wearing more androgynous clothing. None of this matters to her husband, who she said has always affirmed her as a woman but is also sensitive to ways in which her dysphoria could spike in some social situations.

Bryn is a seventeen-year-old adolescent who identifies as gender nonbinary and prefers gender-neutral pronouns (them/them). Bryn has been managing late-onset gender dysphoria for the past year. They identify as a Christian and have turned to specific faith-based spiritual disciplines to deepen their faith. They are most drawn to corporate worship, adoration, reading of Scripture, prayer, and service to others. Bryn dresses in more androgynous attire and has no current interest in hormone therapy because they are not sure how they would respond to developing a "cross-gender" identity, which they think would be as problematic as adopting a gender identity in keeping with their birth sex.

These three stories of gender-diverse presentations represent different ways people have managed their gender dysphoria or gender-identity conflicts. Candace has made a medical transition through the use of hormone therapy (HT). She will have to take these hormones regularly for the rest of her life to maintain their clinical effects, which is an expensive commitment, but Candace believes it has been worth it. Morgan is using various adaptive coping strategies (for example, how she keeps her hair) to help her manage her dysphoria while presenting as a woman. Bryn identifies as gender nonbinary and is finding faith-based coping strategies helpful. Bryn values androgynous attire and gender-neutral pronouns and appears to have reached a place of peace in terms of managing gender dysphoria.

The approach we take in therapy and consultations with older adolescents and adults is summarized in figure 14.1. We are initially trying to determine whether the diagnosis of Gender Dysphoria is warranted. To confirm this diagnosis, we rule out gender-atypical expression that perhaps violates cultural norms for sex and gender but does not warrant a gender dysphoria diagnosis. We also rule out psychosis, body dysmorphic disorder, and transvestic fetishism. This diagnostic process occurs in the early stage of therapy. We are likely already aware of the management strategies our clients have used or are using since these come up during assessment and are often part of how clients present and interact with us.

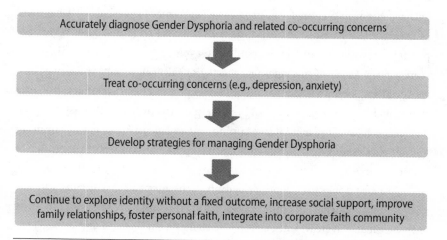

Figure 14.1. General flow of care with older adolescents and adults

We also recognize that people who experience gender dysphoria are at heightened risk for other concerns so we try to make an accurate diagnosis of any co-occurring concerns. When co-occurring concerns (such as depressive or anxiety disorders) are present, we focus on treating those concerns first unless a client's gender dysphoria is so difficult to manage that they are in crisis and we need to explore management strategies right away.

Once we have diagnosed and treated any co-occurring concerns, we then return in earnest to management strategies for gender dysphoria. In our experience, people navigating gender identity and faith will turn to various strategies in an attempt to manage their gender dysphoria or explore their sense of gender identity and expression. We view these strategies as residing along a continuum, and one of our counseling goals is to help clients determine their place along that continuum.

Throughout the course of therapy, as we work with clients in a stepwise fashion to identify and incorporate various management strategies, we are also helping clients explore gender identity without a fixed outcome; explore how their gender identity and faith identity are related (including their personal faith and participation in a local, corporate faith community); increase social support, which can include disclosure; and improve family relationships that may have been strained by gender-identity exploration.

We do not have an exhaustive list of management strategies. However, we have seen many creative management strategies employed, and we have organized them in a chart from least invasive to most invasive. This measure of invasiveness roughly corresponds with how WPATH discusses reversible, partially reversible, and irreversible interventions (Coleman et al., 2012). Here are the kinds of management strategies (although not exhaustive) that we see along a continuum: (a) identify and process negative affect, utilizing dialectical behavior therapy (DBT) principles; (b) utilize faith-based coping strategies; (c) engage in adaptive coping; (d) engage in cross-gender or other gender expression; (e) engage in adaptive coping and adopt transgender or other diverse gender identities; (f) pursue a complete social transition; (g) begin low-dose cross-gender hormones; (h) adopt a cross-gender identity with medical (hormonal) intervention; and (i) adopt a cross-gender identity with medical (surgical) intervention. (See fig. 14.2.)

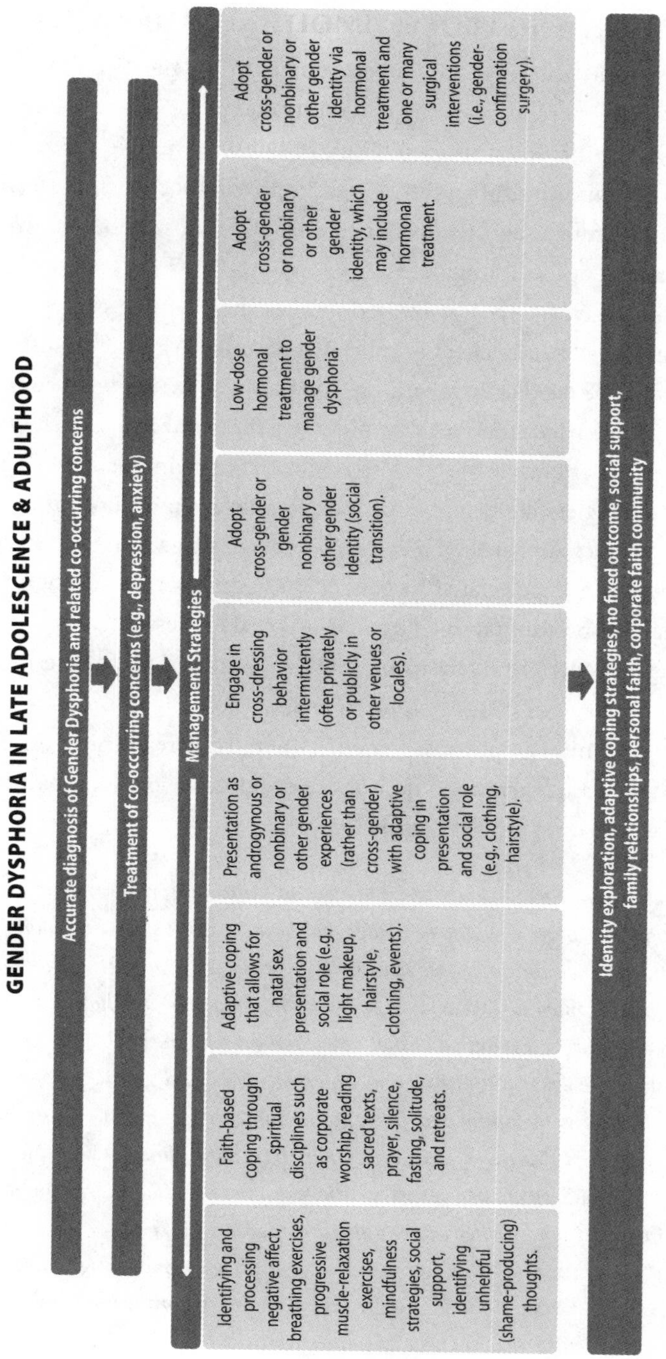

GENDER DYSPHORIA IN LATE ADOLESCENCE & ADULTHOOD

Accurate diagnosis of Gender Dysphoria and related co-occurring concerns

Treatment of co-occurring concerns (e.g., depression, anxiety)

Management Strategies

Identifying and processing negative affect, breathing exercises, progressive muscle-relaxation exercises, mindfulness strategies, social support, identifying unhelpful (shame-producing) thoughts.	Faith-based coping through spiritual disciplines such as corporate worship, reading sacred texts, prayer, silence, fasting, solitude, and retreats.	Adaptive coping that allows for natal sex presentation and social role (e.g., light makeup, hairstyle, clothing, events).	Presentation as androgynous or nonbinary or other gender experiences (rather than cross-gender) with adaptive coping in presentation and social role (e.g., clothing, hairstyle).	Engage in cross-dressing behavior intermittently (often privately or publicly in other venues or locales).	Adopt cross-gender or gender nonbinary or other gender identity (social transition).	Low-dose hormonal treatment to manage gender dysphoria.

Adopt cross-gender or nonbinary or other gender identity, which may include hormonal treatment.	Adopt cross-gender or nonbinary or other gender identity via hormonal treatment and one or many surgical interventions (i.e., gender-confirmation surgery).

Identity exploration, adaptive coping strategies, no fixed outcome, social support, family relationships, personal faith, corporate faith community

Figure 14.2. Management strategies along a continuum

IDENTIFICATION AND PROCESSING OF NEGATIVE AFFECT

This first strategy has almost certainly been employed by most clients even before they come to therapy. Learning to identify and process negative affect can include performing breathing exercises, progressive muscle-relaxation exercises, and various mindfulness strategies; improving social support; and identifying unhelpful thoughts in order to challenge those thoughts with more helpful and adaptive thoughts.

Because clients have likely already tried some of these coping strategies, it is important not to assume a client is entirely unfamiliar with them. Instead of asking if they have tried deep breathing, you may want to ask what coping strategies they have tried, then let them identify the strategies and share a little about their experience using these strategies. It is also important to keep in mind that strategies like progressive muscle relaxation do not decrease gender dysphoria per se, but they may help clients manage some aspects of the stress they experience related to gender incongruence, including how other people are responding to their gender-atypical expressions.

Even though clients are likely to be familiar with some of these basic coping strategies they can still be helpful to review. Most clients only use one or two of the techniques and can benefit either from relearning an old strategy—and perhaps learning to do it more effectively—or from learning a new strategy they were not yet familiar with.

Kris is a sixty-four-year-old male-to-female transgender person who came in seeking help for her marriage. The marriage had been strained since Kris made the decision to transition two years ago. Kris's wife declined to participate in therapy, but Kris wanted to have a place to discuss her marriage and how best to relate to her wife during this difficult time. After taking a relationship history and problem history, we learned that Kris was experiencing several symptoms of depression and anxiety, including depressed mood, difficulty with concentration, sleep disruption, and decreased pleasure in activities that ordinarily were pleasurable to her. While we created a therapeutic space for Kris to explore how to improve her relationship with her wife, we also provided her with psychoeducation on sleep hygiene and taught her several coping strategies, including a deep breathing exercise she could practice daily and a progressive muscle-relaxation technique for moments when she felt especially stressed at home.

DBT PRINCIPLES

Colleen Sloan and Danielle Berke (2018) offer a helpful chapter on incorporating DBT principles in therapeutic work with transgender clients. They rightfully acknowledge that studies have not been provided to date regarding the efficacy of this treatment for gender dysphoria as such. Still, they point out that the distress around gender can be heightened due to emotional dysregulation and ineffective efforts to cope that lead to externalizing behaviors, including substance abuse and risky sexual behaviors. The authors offer a fascinating account of the ways that invalidating environments both in one's family of origin and in one's society at large can present immense challenges to transgender clients. These challenges can make it difficult to learn how to "label, understand, tolerate, modulate and use emotions to organize effective behavior" (Sloan & Berke, 2018, p. 125). This only further complicates the process of developing a stable sense of personhood and identity, which makes the introduction of DBT principles critical to working with clients who want to make changes that allow them to be more effective in their lives and relationships. Incorporating acceptance and change, dialectics, synthesis, problem solving, and a nonjudgmental stance are all indicated to assist in this process. Group work could also be effective in order to incorporate DBT skills and bolster insight as well as a sense of community for clients.

FAITH-BASED COPING STRATEGIES

Most of the clients we see come from a religious faith tradition that is important to them. Their faith tradition often brings additional layers of complexity to their navigation of gender identity. However, conventionally religious clients also bring with them a rich history of coping resources that may be considered in therapy. Granted, it can also be challenging to incorporate religiously congruent interventions into therapy, but many of our clients want to find a way to do just that. Faith-based coping strategies can include reading sacred texts (for example, the Bible) and engaging in contemplative prayer, silence, fasting, solitude, spiritual retreats, service to others, and corporate worship.

Sara is a fifty-year-old male-to-female transgender person who transitioned several years before we met her. Although we did not know her as a client, we have enjoyed her acquaintance for several years. Sara confided in us about her faith journey and some of the decisions she faced in navigating gender dysphoria. Due to the strength of her dysphoria, she ultimately chose to medically transition. Sara shared with us how important it was to her to be part of a local church. She deeply valued corporate worship and service to others. The church she attended was sorting out its own policies related to gender identity and expression, and it was not always an ideal fit for Sara. What she found helpful was to invest in an area of ministry that the church struggled to fill: work with the homeless. Sara was particularly drawn to those on the margins who were in the greatest need. She found that serving the homeless was a source of encouragement to her and provided her with a meaningful pathway to be a part of her corporate faith community. Her investment in homeless ministry reflected her desire to give to others and to identify with the disenfranchised and marginalized.

One natal female who experiences gender dysphoria and uses her female name and pronouns shared with us in an interview how important service was to her: "Helping other people—focusing on the problems of others. I was created to love God and love people. God made me generous and empathic and that's what matters" (Yarhouse & Houp, 2016, p. 58).

FINDING A PLATEAU

The goal of exploring gender identity—in particular, exploring conflicts between a person's gender identity and their religious identity—is to help each person find their plateau. Clients often feel a pull toward mountaintops presented to them as expected destinations for navigating gender identity. Increasingly, medical interventions—hormonal and/or surgical—are those mountaintops. What we want to help them achieve is not so much a specific destination but a safe, stable plateau where they can thrive. In our experience, many clients do not actually pursue medical interventions in response to gender dysphoria; rather, they identify a plateau where they are able to stabilize in terms of their self-understanding and their use of management strategies.

This idea of helping clients find their plateau relates to our earlier discussion of management strategies residing along a continuum. Different management strategies may represent different plateaus; each person must discern which approach will help them find a settled way of being in the world, a plateau where they can experience greater peace and contentment.

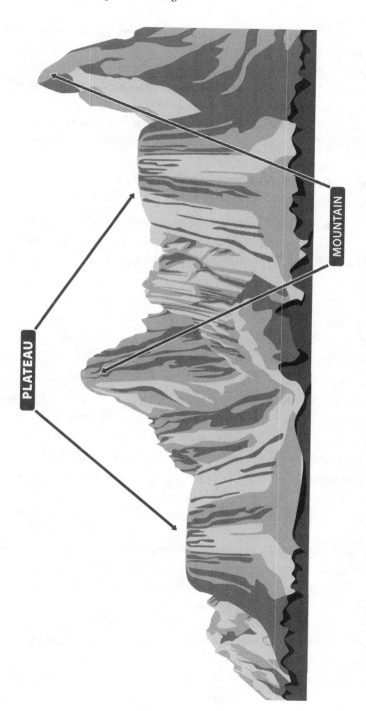

Figure 14.3. Mountaintops and plateaus

Keep in mind that plateaus vary considerably from person to person. What works and is sustainable for one person may not work or achieve the same results (and will therefore not be sustainable) for another person.

Plateaus also vary in duration. A client may plateau at one set of management strategies for six months or six years. Some clients settle into a plateau that they maintain for the rest of their lives. Others find that after a few weeks or months or years they need to revisit their plateau and explore other options.

ADAPTIVE COPING AND NATAL-SEX-GENDER PRESENTATION

Some clients on their own accord have utilized various coping strategies that enable them to present in keeping with their natal sex and social role. For a natal male, these strategies might include keeping his hair longer and wearing light makeup. For a natal female, coping may include keeping her hair shorter, wearing no makeup or other accessories, and wearing a sports bra.

Clients are sometimes drawn to living according to their natal sex and corresponding social role simply because it seems easier within their complex social network and community. They fear rejection. Others are at an age and life stage where the challenges to transition are great and their capacity to manage their distress through adaptive coping is high; these are most often older clients who have been navigating their experience for many years. We have met with many clients who are open to the possibility of transition, but we have also sat with people who truly have no interest in taking such steps and are simply desperate to find ways of managing their dysphoria. They see their dysphoria as an enduring reality, and—like other experiences in their lives—they want to figure out how to deal with it.

Take Elle, a sixty-five-year-old natal female who experiences gender dysphoria. She has struggled with gender dysphoria since childhood but did not have language for this experience. At a young age, she concluded, "I am crazy," and carried on with her life in the best way she knew how. She chose an occupation where she could present in more androgynous attire, for example, by wearing scrubs to work, and simply chose to avoid all women's groups at her church. Although she was immensely relieved when she was diagnosed with Gender Dysphoria—now having language and validation that her experience was "real"—she did not consider many of the strategies that involve cross-sex identification. Her personal

values, her age, her stage in life, and other factors contributed to her lack of in-
terest in these options. She was not seeking contact with the local transgender
community, but she did want to understand how to live with dysphoria in the
body she was born with. She feared going to many therapists because she said,
"What if they try to force me to do something I don't want to do?"

In addition to developing adaptive coping strategies for dysphoria, clients like Elle may have co-occurring concerns to address in therapy as well. With regard to adaptive coping, it is important for clinicians to exude confidence and hope that the strategies clients turn to will actually help. Regardless of whether a client's chosen path involves transition or not, instilling hope is an essential task of therapy. Western culture's dominant depictions of trans-gender people nearly always involve cross-sex identification. This monolithic narrative only creates more difficulty for those who, for any number of reasons, choose not to adopt a cross-sex identity. People who live quietly with gender dysphoria, using adaptive coping strategies, will not likely get the level of celebration portrayed by celebrities or media coverage. Thus, they are a minority within a minority when it comes to support and resources for living with gender dysphoria.

We try to help clients who are developing their coping strategies think about situations, contexts, relationships, and activities that "turn up or down the volume" of their gender dysphoria. Responding to this question can give clients insight into their dysphoria's "exceptions," the times when gender-related distress is not as significant or debilitating. This line of exploration can shed light on coping strategies people have already developed.

Another area to consider is cognitive coping: helping clients to challenge unhelpful beliefs or assumptions about what it means to struggle with an enduring experience such as gender dysphoria. Some clients have taken their dysphoria to mean, "I am not a faithful child of God," "I am not holy enough," or "I have not prayed hard enough for deliverance." Normalizing the struggles people of faith have faced throughout history—struggles with mental and physical illness as well as a range of other forms of suffering—can help a client see that their difficulties do not make them "less than" in the eyes of God.

One task of cognitive coping may be to explore the rigid stereotypes a client has inherited about what it means to be a man or woman. Exploring these stereotypes will also involve challenging negative narratives clients may have heard about natal males who wear long hair and makeup, or about natal females who wear short hair without accessories. Although nonstereotypical behaviors like these are often condemned as unmasculine or unfeminine, clients may find it helpful to recognize that hair length and makeup use do not make a person male or female. When simple coping mechanisms like these are not imbued with moral significance, they become far more effective and sustainable.

INTERMITTENT CROSS-GENDER, GENDER-NONBINARY, OR OTHER GENDER EXPRESSION

Other clients may also present as their natal sex and corresponding social role, but they take additional steps to manage their gender dysphoria or identity. These steps may include intermittent cross-dressing, which could occur privately (as when a natal male wears female undergarments). They may also occur in locations outside a person's regular community, as when someone travels to another city on occasion to cross-dress.

> *Earl, a forty-eight-year-old pastor in the Southern Baptist denomination, came for a consultation on gender identity. He reported having struggled with gender dysphoria since he was a child, although he did not know what it was or have the language to describe it for many years. Earl preferred to wear his hair as long as possible (without drawing attention to himself), but he found that his public role limited what he could do publicly to manage his dysphoria. He discovered, however, that intermittent cross-dressing seemed to help him manage his dysphoria. He did this privately, about once every other week, and it seemed to "take the edge off" of a distress that ebbed and flowed. During our consultation, Earl's wife was tearful at times. She wanted Earl to experience peace from his internal conflict, and she wanted peace for herself as well. She hated to see her husband so "tied up in knots" from time to time. Although she didn't like Earl's cross-dressing, she said he was discreet and private. What mattered most to her was that this coping mechanism was helpful to him, which made everything else a little easier.*

ADAPTIVE COPING AND ANDROGYNOUS, NONBINARY, OR OTHER GENDER EXPERIENCE

Some clients may choose to utilize adaptive coping while presenting (either publicly or privately) as a gender other than their natal sex. Rather than adopt a cross-gender identity, they might instead identify as androgynous, gender nonbinary, or another gender-diverse presentation.

Emma is a natal female who publicly identifies as a woman (in part because of the local faith community of which she is a part) but privately identifies, only to herself, as transgender. She shared with us,

> I dress a certain way to manage my dysphoria. Dressing as a tomboy helps. It's easier for female-to-male. I avoid situations when I would be expected to wear a dress—situations with heightened gender expectations. Black-tie events. I understand which situations push my buttons and avoid them. (Yarhouse & Houp, 2016, p. 58)

ADAPTIVE COPING AND CROSS-GENDER, GENDER-NONBINARY, OR OTHER GENDER IDENTITY

Clients may also elect to adopt a cross-gender, gender-nonbinary, or other gender identity through a social transition. This means that, in essentially every sphere of life, they present and are known as the cross-gender identity or other gender identity they experience themselves to be.

> *Kallie, age eighteen, was relieved when his mother and father allowed him to adopt a cross-gender identity by making a social transition when he went off to college. Kallie, who would now be known as Cal, had been in therapy for the past three years exploring gender identity and dealing with the ups and downs of gender dysphoria. He had known others who had opted for medical interventions, but he was wary of taking on "too much, too soon." He was concerned, too, that he might burn a bridge to his parents, who loved him and wanted him to pace himself. But to go to college and present as Cal, to have the opportunity to make a new start at school, seemed to hold so much promise and possibility. He was relieved and grateful. At the end-of-semester break that next year, Cal stopped in to say that he was doing well, that classes were challenging, and that the decision to socially transition seemed like a good decision so far. This was a manageable "plateau" that seemed to be addressing his main concerns.*

Another example of how this step can manifest is in anticipation of puberty. While this chapter is primarily focused on coping for adults, it is important to highlight the way this means of coping can manifest in a prepubescent child.

Shay is a natural male who is eleven years old and has experienced gender dys-
phoria since an early age. Shay has struggled immensely with coping with
physical dysphoria around anatomy and intense fear of the anticipated expe-
rience of puberty. Shay is an example of a person whose physical dysphoria was
so high that she would scream and cry late into the nights about three nights per
week in anticipation of bodily changes. Shay and her parents went to family
therapy and met with a medical provider to consider the option of puberty-
blocking hormones, but they had chosen not to do so at this time as a family, and
Shay's bouts of anger and grief about puberty continued to heighten. When Shay
and her parents decided instead to assist her in a full social transition where she
would present as transgender and make adjustments to her name and pronouns
at home and school simultaneously, and especially once both parents began uti-
lizing the name "Shay" and she/her/hers pronouns, Shay's episodes of physical
dysphoria ceased, and she reported feeling "happy and no longer depressed" for
the first time in two years.

LOW-DOSE HORMONE USE

Some clients elect to use HT but do so at a lower dose than the normal
clinical dose. They have already made a social transition and are known by
others in their cross-gender or other gender presentation, but they want to
start with a low dose of hormones in order to experience a more gradual
physical change. It is important for clients to speak with their medical provider about any side effects and to understand that low doses of hormones
will still have clinical effects, even though these effects will take longer to
become noticeable.

Tim is a twenty-year-old sophomore in college. Tim was born female and had not
shown signs of gender dysphoria until age seventeen. He admitted to his parents
that he was trans after being confronted by his mother over an Instagram picture
in which he was dressed in stereotypically male attire. Tim and his parents had
a fairly high-conflict relationship over the next year and a half. He pushed hard
for HT, but his parents refused. He was distraught. So were his parents. Tim
made a social transition when he began college. He continued to express a desire
for HT but abided by his parents' wish that he not take any medical steps until
meeting with a mental health professional who had some training in gender
identity. He spent his first eighteen months at college meeting with a counselor.
They worked on exploring his gender identity, developing social support, ex-
ploring his religious faith, and managing his own emotions and gender dysphoria.

He revisited with his parents his desire for HT, and his parents agreed to support the use of low-dose hormones.

As we indicated above, the use of low-dose HT will still have clinical effects, but these effects will take longer to become visible. This gradual process was helpful to Tim and his parents as it gave everyone a little more time to adjust to the changes that were occurring. Of course, many people (like Tim and his parents) will have fundamental disagreements about whether such steps are morally permissible, and some may ultimately refuse to support a decision like Tim's. In Tim's case, however, the gradual nature of the change made it easier for him to reach a compromise with his parents.

The gradual nature of this approach was also important to Kris, whom we mentioned above. Recall that Kris is a sixty-four-year-old male-to-female transgender person who had transitioned two years earlier. She shared with us that when she began hormone treatment, she chose to use a low dose, both because she was wary of medical interventions and because she wanted to be sensitive to how any physical changes would be experienced by her wife. After all, there was much grief and interpersonal trauma to be processed in their marriage, and Kris did not want to exacerbate her wife's pain. The hormonal treatment did have a feminizing effect, of course, but it was more gradual and took quite a bit longer to become visible. Kris indicated that the extended timeline was a better fit in terms of the challenges she anticipated (and experienced) in her marriage, as well as in terms of her own reservations about whether such steps would truly relieve her distress or be "worth it" when counting the cost of the conflict in her marriage.

ADOPTION OF CROSS-GENDER, GENDER-NONBINARY, OR OTHER GENDER IDENTITY WITH MEDICAL (HORMONAL) INTERVENTION

This strategy is identical to the previous one, except that those who adopt a cross-gender or other gender presentation and elect to begin HT, do so at a clinical dose and so experience physical changes in a shorter time (where experiences like facial hair growth, voice deepening, and breast growth can take two or more years to see a full effect). These clients have typically already made a social transition that is being further consolidated through the use of medical intervention in the form of HT. Again, it is important for clients to work closely with their medical provider to discuss side effects, to understand how the hormone regimen works, and so on. To achieve clinical effects, HT must be used for the rest of a person's life. Since these hormones can be expensive, taking this step can introduce a set of challenges different from the challenges that usually accompany the preceding coping strategies.

In *Understanding Gender Dysphoria*, Yarhouse introduced readers to Blake, age twenty-eight, a female-to-male transgender person who was raised in a Christian family and who made the difficult decision to pursue medical support in transition. Blake shared in an interview that the word *transitioning* can be misunderstood to mean that everyone takes all the same steps to adopt a cross-gender identity. Not so, Blake explained: "Each person considers what transitioning is for that person" (Yarhouse, 2015, p. 126). For Blake, transitioning included the use of hormones at the time of the interview. Much of the wrestling had taken place for months prior to Blake's decision to begin HT. Blake wrestled with what was morally permissible and how his family and extended family would respond. He also weighed reports on various side effects and the reality that he would have to continue taking hormones for his entire life in order to keep receiving their clinical effects.

ADOPTION OF CROSS-GENDER, NONBINARY, OR OTHER GENDER IDENTITY WITH MEDICAL (SURGICAL) INTERVENTION

Finally, some clients elect to use gender-confirmation surgery (previously referred to as sex-reassignment surgery). Gender-confirmation surgery is not a single surgical procedure. Rather, there are many procedures a person might consider. Some of these procedures involve the removal of primary sex characteristics (like breasts or penis) while others involve the surgical implantation or construction of these sex characteristics. Most people who pursue surgical intervention have already begun HT. However, some people who identify as gender nonbinary or otherwise do not experience a cross-gender identity may consider surgical procedures without utilizing HT. In these cases, although they are not adopting a cross-gender identity, they may still experience primary sex characteristics as distressing and wish to remove these sex characteristics in order to alleviate dysphoria. Some transgender persons may pursue surgical procedures (e.g., chest reconstruction) without pursuing HT. (See fig. 14.4 for an illustration of the various approaches.)

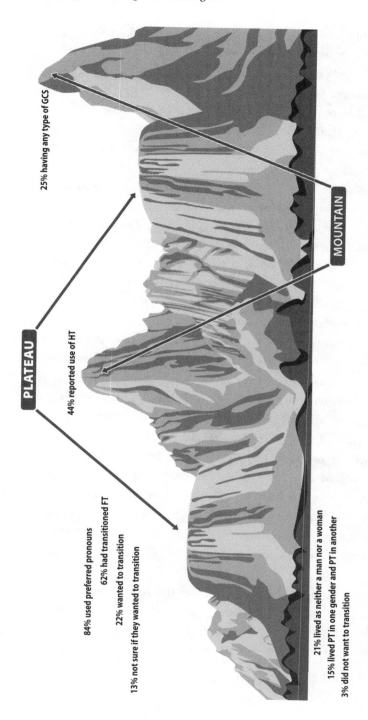

PLATEAU

84% used preferred pronouns
62% had transitioned FT
22% wanted to transition
13% not sure if they wanted to transition

21% lived as neither a man nor a woman
15% lived PT in one gender and PT in another
3% did not want to transition

44% reported use of HT

25% having any type of GCS

MOUNTAIN

Figure 14.4. Mountaintops and plateaus: recent percentages. The illustration of mountaintops and plateaus may be further enhanced by filling in data from the U.S. Transgender Survey in terms of the percentages of adults reporting on how they present to others, as well as how common it was to use preferred pronouns, make a social transition, initiate hormone treatment, or have any type of gender-confirmation surgery. It should be noted that 3% of participants identified as cross-dressers and 35% of participants identified as nonbinary persons. A higher percentage of respondents who identified as cross-dressers and nonbinary did not wish to transition or were unsure if they wished to transition (see James et al., 2016, figure 4.8, p. 47). In the report "transitioning" referred to "the process of living full time in a gender that is different than that on one's original birth certificate" (James et al., 2016, p. 47).

Let's return to Blake, who (as we mentioned previously) is a female-to-male transgender person in his late twenties. Blake's decision to make a medical transition included not only the use of HT but also chest-reconstruction surgery. At the time of our interview, Blake's chest-reconstruction surgery was completed but no other surgical procedures had been pursued. We were impressed by the amount of thought Blake put into weighing this decision and its implications for his relationship with God and others, especially his family and his broader network of community.

Recall that you are helping clients find their plateau. The plateau is the management strategy that is least invasive and provides clients with sufficient relief from dysphoria to be stable and safe. We hope that the analogy of peaks and plateaus is helpful to you and to your clients. Remember that clients may plateau for weeks or months or years; any plateau can be revisited for any number of reasons, and therapy must be a safe place to explore a client's experience with their current (or former) plateau.

It is also recommended that clinicians assist clients in incorporating principles such as acceptance around the possible persistence of gender dysphoria or undesired outcomes when utilizing hormones, pursuing surgeries, etc. (Sloan & Berke, 2018). We clinicians can assist our clients in recognizing that interventions centered around change have their limitations, which allows for the space to hold radical acceptance within these changes and the freedom to optimally adjust to life circumstances, even undesirable ones.

In the end, we recognize that therapy rarely concludes with every question in a person's life resolved or every outcome achieved. The same is undoubtedly true here. We are honored to bear witness to select chapters of our clients' lives, holding in mind that even along a plateau their journey continues on. The conclusion of therapy involves normalizing this reality, inviting the questions that still have no answers, and honoring what has been accomplished along the way.

In the final section of this book, we offer several real-life examples of therapy around the intersection of gender identity and faith. We hope these examples emphasize the complexity, nuance, and unique challenges that await as you assist clients in navigating this terrain.

PART 4

CASE STUDIES

15

INDIVIDUAL

The Case of Kelly

BACKGROUND

Kelly is an eighteen-year-old Caucasian natal female who presented to individual therapy at our clinic when he had just turned seventeen years old.[1] He identified as agnostic, although he was raised in a conservative Christian home. His parents identified as Pentecostal Christian and reported significant concern and confusion related to Kelly's report of gender-identity questions. Kelly received individual therapy with adjunctive collateral sessions with parents and one of his siblings for one year. The focus of this treatment was primarily on assessing for gender dysphoria, referral to a specialty clinic to pursue options to manage distress, addressing co-occurring anxiety and panic symptoms, increasing assertiveness, and facilitating exploration and expression of affect in therapy. Kelly returned to our clinic to continue services several months after ending the first course of therapy. The focus of this second treatment was to continue exploring gender identity in order to prepare Kelly to reevaluate pathways moving forward.

ETHICAL CONSIDERATIONS

When working with minors, we want to distinguish between consent and assent. Consent is what parents were able to give for Kelly because he was still a minor when he came to therapy. Assent is what we always request from a minor, especially when the work they are doing is around gender identity. Gender is a sensitive topic, and we wanted Kelly to be invested in the treatment and to feel comfortable with an approach that allowed him to explore gender identity.

---

[1] Kelly currently identifies as transgender, and male pronouns will be utilized in this case study.

We also wanted a young person like Kelly and his parents to appreciate the difference between confidentiality and privacy. We explained to Kelly and his parents, both separately and together, the limits of confidentiality. That is, we would need to disclose information to appropriate authorities and parents if Kelly shared about risk of imminent harm to himself or another identified person. We would also need to report abuse of a child or dependent adult, as well as comply with legal demands in situations where information was subpoenaed by a lawyer to be presented to a court. However, privacy allows the therapist to discreetly manage information that emerges from individual sessions. For example, parents who agree to privacy for their child's counseling would choose not to exercise their right to access notes from previous counseling sessions. Kelly's father often called the clinic to ask for information about what Kelly was saying in session. We shared with the family that, insofar as parents took a more hands-on role in the content of sessions, this lack of privacy may lead Kelly to withhold information. Insofar as the parents were able and willing to allow session content to be private, even though they legally had access to Kelly's file, we encouraged them that this strategy may help Kelly feel more freedom to share openly in sessions. As he grew more comfortable and developed trust, we explained, he may begin sharing information with them of his own accord.

Because we worked with Kelly in the context of a specialty clinic where the parents were also receiving couples therapy for themselves, we needed to ensure releases of information between various therapists to be able to discreetly discuss individual cases when these conversations were in the best interest of the family.

Kelly turned eighteen through the course of therapy. Because of this, he needed to sign new consent documents for his own treatment and to decide what information he would allow to be released to his parents. Since Kelly's parents had already been so actively involved in his treatment, and because he wanted their support in decision making moving forward, he was ready and willing to consent to their continued access to his information. We could certainly imagine circumstances where this would not have been the case.

PHASE ONE—ASSESSMENT AND TREATMENT PLANNING

An important piece of work around gender identity is appreciating the necessity of assessment prior to treatment planning. In Kelly's case, his parents brought him to us because they wanted him to explore gender identity in a faith-based clinic. We began by educating the parents and Kelly about how our approach emphasizes assessing for mood symptoms and other symptoms that may impede a person's capacity to explore gender identity. This meant looking for mental health concerns such as anxiety and depressive symptoms. We did not want Kelly making decisions about gender identity out of a depressed mood state, for instance. Kelly's parents agreed to this; it was clear that Kelly was struggling with anxiety and depressive symptoms, including passive suicidal ideation.

Since Kelly was a minor, we spent some of our initial sessions meeting with Kelly and his parents together. This allowed us to appreciate, from a family systems perspective, how Kelly and his parents related, communicated, and discussed matters related to gender identity and faith. We even had one of Kelly's siblings, the one he was closest to, join for several sessions to improve the communication in that relationship.

An additional area of assessment relates to the intersection of gender identity and religious identity. In this book we have given you a range of questions to use for this purpose. Even though Kelly was a self-professed agnostic, he believed it was important to understand how his gender-identity exploration could be impacted by the faith he was raised in. He still joined his parents for weekly church services and had several friends in the church's youth group. His agnosticism as a belief system was new to him, and it was evident from our assessment that spiritual values were still an important part of Kelly's life. Kelly was also very close to his parents and one of his siblings. He wanted to have their support throughout his life, and the fact that faith was an integral part of their lives made spiritual identity worth exploring.

PHASE TWO—STABILIZING MOOD SYMPTOMS

We began by working toward stabilizing Kelly's mood state. Since this was his first time in therapy, we introduced foundational skills for coping with distress that would transfer and be applicable to the work he would later do around gender identity. Using cognitive behavioral therapy interventions and mindfulness skills, we increased Kelly's adaptive coping and helped him gain insight into the triggers for his various mood states. We also engaged in safety planning early on, knowing that mood symptoms can increase while exploring gender identity in therapy. We wanted to have a plan in place if Kelly's suicidal thoughts were to become more active, especially since these symptoms can change on a daily basis.

Although Kelly's parents were initially in support of focusing on mood, they became increasingly frustrated about the way therapy was not primarily attending to gender identity. They reported wanting to shift the focus of treatment away from anxiety and depression. This required additional psychoeducation about how important it is to attend to mood symptoms first. Ultimately, we were able to begin incorporating some gender-related exploration in the mix as well. We reprioritized addressing depressive symptoms when Kelly's suicidal thoughts returned after a hiatus of several months. Parents agreed that this was the appropriate move because suicidal thoughts jeopardized Kelly's overall functioning in many areas of life and sense of safety. Therapy also helped Kelly begin to develop emotional intelligence since he was initially wary of expressing emotions about anything, let alone gender identity.

PHASE THREE—EXPLORATION OF GENDER IDENTITY

Once Kelly's co-occurring mood symptoms had been assessed and addressed, he was in a much better position to explore gender identity, and we were able to understand him more fully to assist him on this journey.

An important aspect of care here was assessing for Gender Dysphoria. This was especially important as Kelly was considering possible pharmacological interventions to address gender-identity distress and potentially assist him in a social transition. When it came to diagnosis, Kelly reported and clearly experienced gender-related distress. Kelly's case was distinct from the typical gender dysphoria presentation, though, in that he denied any gender-related distress prior to around the age of fourteen. This was a newer experience, and one Kelly's parents didn't quite understand. His parents were concerned about whether Kelly was being influenced by peers at school since he was a member of various groups such as theater and band that included many peers exploring gender identity. At the same time, Kelly's distress around gender was not something he spoke about openly; in fact, he struggled to convey emotions in therapy in general. This was another reason it was important to help him develop an emotional vocabulary and rapport in therapy prior to delving into work related to gender-identity exploration.

In therapy, we used a range of diagnostic assessments to determine the presence of gender dysphoria. Since Kelly did not meet criteria in childhood, it was evident that his was not an early-onset case. Still, Kelly did meet criteria for a Gender Dysphoria diagnosis in adolescence and adulthood.

One of the challenges at this time was educating Kelly and his parents about the diagnosis of Gender Dysphoria and what it meant and didn't mean. We shared with Kelly and his parents that Kelly's distress around gender was clearly impacting his academic and social functioning, even after accounting for and treating mood symptoms.

We drew from a range of interventions to help facilitate gender-identity exploration, including many of those already mentioned in this book. Kelly, an excellent artist, began by developing diagrams of all the gender options he could think of (male, female, trans male, trans female, nonbinary, gender-fluid, and so on). This first step allowed Kelly to understand not only his theoretical understanding of gender but also the personal meaning he attributed to labels and identities.

For Kelly, a significant piece of trans male identity was the rigid narratives he experienced surrounding femininity, both in the faith community where he was raised and in the broader culture. Trans male identity became a perceived pathway to confidence, representing the ability to reject these narratives and choose his own identity. As Kelly used art to reflect on his understanding of gender, it became evident that the images of what it meant to be female or a woman were drawn in depressed, sad, and marginalized ways. Images conveying what it meant to be male or a man were drawn with a happy mood and in an active way.

At the time Kelly was exploring gender more deeply, he was also exhibiting greater differentiation from his parents. He was turning eighteen, which meant he was considering decisions about college, majors, and even the possibility of a full social transition with hormones. Up until this point, Kelly had struggled to assert himself with his parents. His father was actively involved in his school and therapy in a way that felt stifling to him. His parents eventually realized during their own process of couples therapy that the father's overfunctioning was a tool for managing the anxiety he felt about

Kelly's unknown future. In the midst of exploring gender, we also supported Kelly in practicing assertive communication and engaging in boundary setting appropriate to his age.

PHASE FOUR—WEIGHING DECISIONS

In this phase of therapy, our work involved ongoing consultation with an endocrinologist and social worker from whom Kelly was seeking care at a local specialty clinic. Kelly was weighing the implications of taking testosterone to promote a social transition. He used his therapy sessions with us to discuss the permanence of hormone therapy, its impact on fertility, its other side effects, and its potential impact on his family system.

It was also evident that the possibility of not beginning hormones was a source of stress for Kelly. He was struggling with motivation to complete school assignments, and his passive suicidal ideation had become more active. We returned to safety planning as it had been some time since we developed the original plan. We did further work around mood functioning in order to determine if Kelly was in a stable place to move forward with decisions about hormone therapy.

Kelly's parents were involved in their own couples therapy at this time, processing their reactions and concerns around Kelly's gender-identity exploration. They had major reservations about Kelly's choice to pursue hormone therapy. At the same time, they were positioning themselves to accompany Kelly along whatever path he chose, so long as there was also opportunity to voice their concerns.

In terms of the current plateau as Kelly began hormone therapy, we used therapy as a space to monitor his mood and his functioning as well as his distress related to gender identity. Kelly was demonstrating greater self-confidence and self-determination over the course of therapy, and as he received hormone therapy he reported that gender-related distress subsided significantly. He did not think he would be interested in more irreversible interventions, such as a range of surgeries, but was establishing a level of comfort with the interventions he had sought thus far.

PHASE FIVE—CONSOLIDATING THE GAINS OF THERAPY

Several months after Kelly began hormone therapy, he was preparing to move to college. He was working on communicating with his parents appropriately, engaging in activities that would help maintain his mood and functioning, and setting up individual therapy while at school. In addition, he was developing a community of peers through a summer course prior to starting college that fall.

We were able to use this time to consolidate the gains Kelly had made in therapy and to hear from him how he felt he had grown and matured over the course of therapy. Kelly certainly felt a greater sense of congruence related to gender identity and was also reporting improved relationships with his parents. He had been able to set boundaries with his parents when needed as he was differentiating more and launching to college, but he was also able to hear their perspective and questions about his future in a much less defensive way.

FINAL REFLECTIONS

We want to note that, in addition to individual therapy with Kelly, much of our work involved ensuring that Kelly's parents had adequate support for their own process. They received couples therapy at our clinic, creating space for them to wrestle with their own questions around their child's gender identity and to cope with their reactions. We also provided them with a referral for a LGBTQ+ parent supportive group, a space designed for parents of LGBTQ+ youth to process their difficulties and questions with others. These support measures helped immensely in attending to the parents' needs while allowing Kelly to do his own work in individual therapy. Kelly's parents were much more able to support Kelly's exploration when they were given spaces to manage their own reactions and experiences related to this process.

We were able to communicate with Kelly's parents' pastor at times, with their consent, to offer recommendations for the pastor to help the parents in their journey. We also helped the parents think through how and when to handle disclosure to friends about what their family was navigating. It was important that Kelly was on board with these steps as well so that disclosures were not occurring without his knowledge. The more the family framed this process as a journey they were on together, the more cohesive they became.

16

COUPLES THERAPY

The Case of Ben (Bea) and Elodie

BACKGROUND

Ben, age fifty-five, and Elodie, age fifty-three, are a Caucasian couple who asked to be seen for marital therapy in light of Ben's recent disclosure of gender dysphoria.[1] Ben and Elodie both identify as Christians. They have been active in a local Presbyterian church, where they raised two children who are now adults and out of the home. Neither of their adult children are aware of Ben's gender dysphoria. Ben has been in individual therapy for the past two years with a clinician he describes as "nice and generally helpful and knowledgeable about general mental health concerns, but he has no experience with transgender people." Elodie is also in therapy following Ben's disclosure of gender dysphoria. She says of herself, "I'm already prone to anxiety, and I just thought I should talk to someone. I have no idea where we are headed." The focus of marital therapy was to discuss together the impact of gender dysphoria on them as a couple.

ETHICAL CONSIDERATIONS

One issue to address when working with couples is how to handle confidentiality. When people come to therapy, they share private information in exchange for mental health services. That private information is kept confidential. That is, clients can expect that such information will not ordinarily be shared with others, although there are various exceptions, such as mandatory reporting of child abuse.

---

[1]We will use male pronouns with reference to Ben and female pronouns with reference to Bea in this case study. The case itself combines elements from several couples we have seen so as to further mask identities.

Confidentiality takes on a special meaning when working with couples. Clinicians have to determine how they will approach the privacy of what either spouse shares with the clinician when the other spouse is not present, perhaps in an individual session or over the phone. For example, Elodie would at times call the clinic and ask that a topic be brought up in our next couples session. We encouraged Elodie to bring that concern to the next session and articulate it for herself rather than asking her therapist to bring it up. This way, we could honor the privacy of Elodie's request without damaging Ben's trust.

Another issue that arises with couples has to do with the future of their marriage. It is up to the couple to determine whether they will remain together, separate, or divorce. Mental health professionals may have opinions and recommendations, but ultimately these decisions are made by the individuals who make up the marriage.

PHASE ONE—ASSESSMENT AND TREATMENT PLANNING

Ben came to couples therapy with a diagnosis of Gender Dysphoria made by his current provider. Although that clinician apparently did not have much experience working with transgender persons, he had made the diagnosis, and Ben was satisfied with that. In our work together, Ben did not look for a second opinion; he was working from the standpoint of having received the diagnosis and wanting to consider its implications for their marriage.

We began by reviewing a therapist disclosure form and advanced informed consent form that had been modified for work with couples. We also discussed the importance of identifying and treating co-occurring concerns. Elodie appeared to be struggling with symptoms of depression (e.g., depressed mood, anhedonia), and she was currently seeing an individual therapist who had signed a release form for us to coordinate care. Ben did not appear to have any co-occurring concerns. We also discussed our approach to care at our specialty clinic, the three lenses through which people see gender-identity concerns (i.e., integrity, disability, and diversity), and the idea of identifying the least invasive way of coping with gender dysphoria.

Since Ben and Elodie were married, we assessed their marriage in a number of areas including communication, problem solving, sources of potential conflict (e.g., discussing finances), and sexual intimacy. We also looked at their overall quality of life to get a sense for how they viewed gender-identity concerns in the context of other experiences. Finally, we assessed their religious identities, faith background, and current faith beliefs and practices, particularly how their religious faith informed their understanding of sex, gender, and marriage.

The assessment of their religious identities revealed that both Ben and Elodie were highly religious and viewed their faith as impacting all areas of their lives. They both held a high, covenantal view of marriage. This assessment allowed us to appreciate how Ben and Elodie related to one another and to God with respect to gender identity and faith. At the time of our initial assessments, Ben tended to view his gender dysphoria through a disability lens: he saw himself as having a condition that was likely the result of the fallen world in which we live. In contrast, Elodie initially viewed Ben's concerns through an integrity lens in which Ben's gender dysphoria was a moral problem, a result of his own moral failing rather than a product of the fall or a medical or psychiatric condition.

PHASE TWO—GAUGING ATTITUDES TOWARD GENDER-IDENTITY CONCERNS

We wanted to begin by gauging everyone's attitude toward Ben's gender-identity concerns. Although Ben's views reflected a disability lens at the beginning of our work together, he often slipped into language that reflected a diversity lens. He was comfortable when we referenced his gender dysphoria from a psychological standpoint, but over time he abandoned that diagnostic language to talk more about "who I really am." We began to suspect that this person perhaps already had a name and a sense of identity in Ben's mind. Elodie began therapy with an integrity lens, but she deeply feared that it was "only a matter of time" before Ben would transition completely. The more we spoke together, the more her language softened, shifting away from moral terms of right and wrong and toward compassionate terms of a condition that Ben had to work on or work through. Gender Dysphoria became a real diagnosis in her mind, something she wanted to see resolved for Ben. We utilized a couples approach referred to as the "Relational Restoration Model" (Sells & Yarhouse, 2011), looking at how each partner manages injury and pain and how partners often misread one another's defenses (or ways of managing pain) when they are responding to injury.

By his own admission, Ben was not working with a clinician who had much experience with gender-identity concerns. Ben was encouraged to explore gender identity further with his therapist, which he did to some extent. He would try out different management strategies such as using light makeup and growing his hair longer. These strategies seemed to help him manage his dysphoria for several weeks, after which he asked about other strategies such as the use of cross-sex attire and the possibility of changing his name and pronouns. Elodie did not mind Ben's longer hair, nor did she mind his use of light makeup. She was uncomfortable seeing Ben "in drag," as she initially put it, so Ben was respectful of Elodie's wishes and only cross-dressed when she was not going to be home for extended periods of time.

PHASE THREE—FURTHER EXPLORATION OF GENDER IDENTITY IN MARRIAGE

After performing assessments and discussing the three lenses with Ben and Elodie, we invited them to share with one another how their lenses informed their experience of Ben's gender identity and their expectations for their marriage. We understood that our role did not involve assisting Ben in the direct exploration of his gender identity; this he was doing with his individual therapist. Rather, we would focus on how that exploration was managed in the context of Ben's faith, Elodie's faith, and their marriage. We would assist them on their journey as a couple.

An important aspect of care here was to support both Ben's individual therapy work and Elodie's individual therapy work, recognizing that each individual's needs were markedly different. Ben's individual therapy entailed exploration of gender identity. As for Elodie, she needed a place to process her emotional reactions to Ben's experiences and her questions as a Christian about his suffering, her suffering, and God's view of marriage. What they needed as a couple was a safe, therapeutic space to communicate, process experiences and conflicts, encourage one another, cry together, and demonstrate support for one another.

Since our couples counseling needed to run in parallel tracks with Ben's and Elodie's individual counseling, it was important that we remain in contact with their other counselors and that our sessions be sensitive to changing dynamics in individual counseling. Ben's counseling proved especially impactful on our work, as he reported that existing management strategies were insufficient for his struggles with gender dysphoria. Our clinic provided Ben's individual therapist with a workbook (Yarhouse et al., 2020) we often use with older adolescents and adults navigating gender-identity questions, and Ben reported that he and his individual therapist used selected chapters in their work together. Ben began to travel once a month to explore what it felt like to adopt a cross-gender identity in public for twenty-four or thirty-six hours rather than just three or four hours at a time. Elodie supported this exploration but felt ambivalent, which she shared in our time together: "I want Ben to have these experiences, but I also wish it wasn't needed. I wish what he was already doing [dressing in cross-gender attire for three or four hours or less] was sufficient, because I don't even have to see him that way. I don't think I could handle it. But since he can't manage right now, it would be selfish for me to demand something from him that is so painful."

After a season of adopting an occasional cross-gender identity when Elodie wasn't present, Ben asked if he could share this part of himself with Elodie. Elodie was able to articulate how difficult it would be for her to encounter Ben as a woman, but she also knew that this was an important part of Ben's experience. She loved him and wanted to confront the challenges he and their marriage were facing rather than flee from them. Ben shared with her that he now experienced himself as Bea, a name he had chosen to honor his late sister. Elodie acknowledged that it was hard to meet Bea, but she could also see in Bea something that encouraged her: Bea was more "at ease" and less "irritable" and "sad." This discovery didn't make everything better; in fact, it further complicated their marriage. Elodie did not want to appear to be part of a lesbian couple since this position would violate both of their religious beliefs in terms of what they viewed as morally permissible.

When Ben discussed presenting as Bea, he framed it mostly in terms of the diversity lens. He would talk about how Bea was a part of him he had always known was there, although she had previously been hidden and unexpressed. This shift was hard for Elodie, who experienced Ben's transition to Bea as a loss of someone familiar whom she loved. Elodie framed her husband's situation in terms of the disability lens and felt bad that her husband was in so much pain; she also felt happy for him that he was feeling better. But she was uncomfortable with any language that signaled a diversity lens, which seemed selfish to her. She felt that Ben was selfishly prioritizing himself over their marriage, making the choices he preferred rather than finding a way to cope with or manage the incongruence between his sex and gender identity. She also knew that Ben's improvements were coming at a cost: she would not be able to stay in a marriage with Ben if he were to present full time as Bea.

PHASE FOUR—WEIGHING DECISIONS

In this phase of therapy, Ben and Elodie weighed Ben's decision about whether to present as Ben, Bea, or a combination of the two, and they considered what the future of their marriage would be if Ben chose to transition further toward Bea. They were in conversation with their local pastor, both individually and as a couple. They deeply valued these conversations and were constantly reflecting on how their faith informed their love for one another and what steps would be best to take.

Another important aspect of care here included their family. Ben wanted to share his journey with their adult children. Elodie understood this impulse, but she feared how their children would receive the news, worrying that one or both children would "take sides" in ways that would be divisive. They agreed to write a letter that they could send to their children. This letter was received better than either of them expected. The children reacted differently, but both of them led with love for Ben and Elodie in ways that were thoughtful, mature, patient, and nuanced.

Ben had also begun to consult an endocrinologist and was considering hormone therapy (HT). In terms of finding his current plateau, Ben eventually proceeded with low-dose HT, which allowed any bodily changes to occur gradually over a longer period of time. Elodie was preparing mentally for a separation, which she felt would be necessary. They had made arrangements to live in different physical locations, which was helpful in some ways but also hard for both of them after so many years in the same space. Both Ben and Elodie were encouraged in individual therapy to work on managing this separation and their mood states through the use of cognitive and behavioral interventions. These steps were helpful, but it was a difficult time.

PHASE FIVE—CONSOLIDATING THE GAINS OF THERAPY

Both Bea and Elodie believed that an ongoing physical separation was best for both of them. Neither wished to pursue a divorce, and both wanted to find ways to continue in relationship with each other, but they did not want to return to regular, day-in-and-day-out experiences that might cause further pain and injury. About twelve months after Bea began low-dose hormone therapy, she was beginning to see and experience herself differently. Her body fat was redistributing in ways that made her embodied experience of herself as a woman fit her mental and emotional experience. Elodie was doing better, too, mostly as a result of her individual therapy and the physical separation, which allowed her to support Bea from a distance. They both reported good relationships with their adult children, who managed to find ways to support them without taking sides.

We met for a few additional months to consolidate the gains made in therapy. These were moments for Bea and Elodie to share with one another their experience of physical separation, the conversations each had had with their pastor, and how they were doing in terms of their own spiritual journeys. Bea reported a greater sense of congruence with her gender identity. Both of them were experiencing their ongoing physical separation as a "solution of sorts" to a very complex marriage in which there were no easy answers.

FINAL REFLECTIONS

We have seen couples stay together, separate indefinitely, or divorce. There are no easy answers. Some spouses with gender dysphoria are able to live and present in keeping with their sex recorded at birth. Though this path is painful, they are able to take steps to make it work. They find their plateau. Other spouses are unable to live at that same plateau; they find their way to another management strategy. Sometimes a couple is able to stay together; other times they separate, either in their home or in two different physical locations. Sometimes these separations lead to divorce.

Social support for Christians is often especially thin. Although we could identify a couple of local support groups for Christian couples navigating gender-identity questions, most were so progressive or affirming that they were not a good fit for Ben/Bea and Elodie. This experience can be especially isolating for either or both spouses because no group seems to really get their concerns.

When we are navigating gender identity and faith with couples, there are few conclusions to therapy that seem satisfying to everyone. Marriage therapy is full of concessions, and it is rarely clear which next step is best. That was certainly our experience with Ben/Bea and Elodie. But they were at their best when they were able to grow in their capacity for charity, considering what it could look like to seek the good of their partner.

17

INDIVIDUAL THERAPY

The Case of Rae

BACKGROUND

Rae is a twenty-six-year-old Latina, bisexual, natal female who presented to therapy with disordered eating and gender-related distress and panic symptoms.[1] Rae reported a history of early physical and sexual trauma and gender-related distress that began when she was about three or four years old. Gender-related distress was heightened as she went through puberty, and in any sexual experiences she had in early adulthood. Rae was raised in a Christian home where stereotypically feminine roles were adopted by her mom, and she often got feedback as a child that she "looked like a boy" and "needed to get it together if she was ever going to have a happy life that was blessed by God." Rae came to reject Christian faith as a result but continued to carry immense conflict around spirituality: "If there is a God, he doesn't like me one bit." Rae left home at eighteen and continued to struggle with gender dysphoria, using eating-disorder behaviors to cope with the pain of traumas, low self-worth, panic symptoms, and gender dysphoria. She spoke about how restriction would allow her to numb emotions and escape the "trap" of her body. She also shared about how disordered eating suppressed her secondary sex characteristics and period, thus relieving some of her gender dysphoria. Rae had recently stopped wearing makeup, reporting that it helped with gender dysphoria, and wondered about the need to consider using hormonal therapy or other interventions to help as well.

---

[1]We will use female pronouns with reference to Rae since she utilized she/her/hers pronouns over the course of her treatment.

ETHICAL CONSIDERATIONS

Given Rae's significant history of physical and sexual abuse, a primary concern was evaluating appropriate reports of this when Rae was a minor. This was confirmed through verifying that several Child Protective Services reports had been made.

An additional consideration was discussing advanced informed consent in order to help Rae in determining the appropriateness of the GRIT approach to therapy. We attended to the reality that Rae did not currently subscribe to the beliefs and values of a Christian worldview while acknowledging how much those beliefs continued to influence her gender-identity exploration. She also was still in contact with her family, primarily seeing them on holidays and special occasions, which meant she would continue to step into situations where their particular reactions to her, rooted in their own worldviews, would impact her. She was aware that, even while disavowing the faith she was raised in, she had internalized the messages therein about gender identity to a degree that it would be helpful to draw from this approach in helping her consolidate a gender identity.

PHASE ONE: ASSESSMENT AND TREATMENT PLANNING

As is always the case, we began with assessing current panic symptoms, disordered eating, and gender dysphoria. We used the gender-incongruence scale weekly at the start of our sessions to track her gender-related distress. It was striking to see how much less equipped she was to manage gender dysphoria when her mood states shifted. We prioritized identifying the function of Rae's restrictive eating patterns and helping her disrupt these patterns by involving her in co-occurring intensive outpatient eating-disorder treatment. We acknowledged that weight restoration would likely impact her gender-related distress, and Rae still agreed to focus on restoration to help nourish her mind so that she didn't make decisions around gender identity out of a malnourished state.

In this initial phase, a referral was made for a psychiatrist, although there were clear hesitancies on Rae's part to consider taking medication for panic symptoms. It was clear that we needed to prioritize conversations around this in early treatment because her unmedicated panic symptoms triggered her restrictive eating to cope. She was unable to keep a job at this time due to panic symptoms, and financial stress only exacerbated everything else she was wrestling with.

We also clarified diagnosis of Gender Dysphoria, as Rae had never been formally diagnosed. In order to do so, Rae journaled through gender-identity chapters of her life. She spoke to relevant spiritual messaging in her journal entries and the way the messages from childhood ministry leaders and parents led her to feel great guilt for wrestling with gender identity. She titled and divided her life into chapters related to exploration of gender and identified core themes for each without going into too much detail at that time. This was due to the way traumatic experiences layered in with gender-identity exploration and could become dysregulating. We preemptively practiced grounding skills and other emotional regulation and distress-tolerance skills, anticipating that even identifying these chapters could increase emotional pain for her. As Rae journaled, she began to experience heightened suicidal thoughts, and we used this as validation that stabilization of mood symptoms would be essential prior to continued gender-identity exploration.

Finally, we assessed Rae's religious identity and the impact this identity has had on her exploration of gender identity thus far. We also explored other aspects of identity, including cultural identity, that certainly impacted her sense that "something is wrong with me" for experiencing gender dysphoria. Rae recalled key moments in church growing up, and especially in her home, where Scripture was used as a way to reflect stereotypes that she never felt she could fit into. This led to a sense that there was no way to be a Christian unless she adopted a more "girly" way of being. At the same time, as a child she fondly remembered learning to pray and how nightly prayers were orienting for her. She recalled asking God over and over again to "make me a boy" and becoming increasingly disappointed as she grew and saw that this prayer went unanswered.

PHASE TWO: STABILIZATION OF MOOD SYMPTOMS

This phase began with containment and processing related to memories that emerged as a result of journaling through gender-identity chapters. We integrated a narrative approach to trauma processing, integrating these aspects of experience into a coherent story and making connections between traumatic experiences and the complicated relationship Rae had with her body.

Rae found that utilizing grounding techniques, progressive muscle relaxation, and guided imagery that incorporated safe-place imagery, as well as externalizing safe-place imagery into art projects, helped her establish a sense of safety when flooded with difficult memories of trauma and experiencing heightened gender dysphoria in those moments. Equally important, Rae felt more validated in what had made gender-identity exploration so difficult, recognizing that there had been no "space or safety" to explore gender as a child. This helped Rae soften against her self-critical thoughts that asked, "How have you not figured this out already?"

This phase also included collaborating with a psychiatrist to adjust Rae's medication regimen to assist her in coping with panic symptoms. Rae was able to try a new medication for this after using therapy to explore the barriers to taking consistent medication. This is where cultural humility was important, as Rae initially balked at even learning about possible medications to address her panic symptoms. As she built trust in therapy, she acknowledged the way her Latina family viewed mental health diagnoses as a sign of weakness and signaled that taking medication was "a crutch" and "for crazy people." She said, "When I told my family I was in therapy, their response was to not let anyone put you on medication or you will really be messed up." As she felt empowered to explore gender identity, despite the way it had been shamed in her home, she also gained courage to try medication for panic, ultimately sharing that "it is a game changer" once her panic attacks were better managed. Rae processed the anger she felt at her family of origin for not helping her get on medication sooner, having spent years suffering and turning to maladaptive relationships and coping to manage her mood. As she found her mood increasingly stabilizing, she reported "I can think clearly" and that this opened up possibilities for gender identity that had before not been on the table.

PHASE THREE: RETURNING TO KEY CHAPTERS

Rae called her initial chapter in childhood "Testing the Waters." This is where Rae recalled trying on her brothers' clothing and undergarments; playing with Tonka trucks and hiding Barbies, dolls, and other toys so she "wouldn't have to play with them"; and first stating, "I am supposed to be a boy." The second chapter was titled "Shame and the Storm." Rae recalled many times in early childhood when she was teased around friends and family, especially by her mom, for "trying to be a boy." Rae was punished severely for cutting her hair at age seven because she "hated having long hair." She began to isolate more at that time at school, recalling that she barely talked and she was seen as "odd" by peers and teachers alike. In the third chapter, "Compliance and Conformity," Rae's mother often dressed her in pink dresses, telling her "one way or another you have to get comfortable with this." Rae was brought to sleepovers with girls she did not get along with, and she recalled that her mother would pick out the most stereotypically feminine girls in class to schedule playdates with. Rae would frequently be brought bows and Barbies on birthdays, and her mother would throw away items she found that might be seen as "boy's toys," such as Rae's G.I. Joe collection. The forceful way in which Rae's mom responded to her gender atypicality only alienated Rae more from her parents, siblings, and peers.

As Rae entered puberty, a chapter she titled "The Agony of Changes," Rae recalls consciously choosing to push back on gender stereotypes by wearing dark colors as often as possible, and commenting that, "when I am eighteen I will be whoever I want to be." She said that her period starting felt completely out of her control but that she could control how she dressed despite her parents frequently shaming her for her dress. She entered into chaotic sexual relationships that increased body shame and body disgust. She also began to restrict food intake at that time, finding that it established a sense of control and helped her to lessen the nature of body changes and connectedness to her body.

Rae titled the next chapter "Numbness Takes You Only So Far." This is where her disordered eating increased, as well as exploration with drug use. She worked to numb her distress of all kinds. She retrospectively saw how much these behaviors were ways of coping with gender dysphoria. She lost connection with a higher power of any kind and rejected the consolation of faith, feeling unworthy of any meaningful connections. This brought her to the present day. This chapter she named "Finding Freedom Again." She had already done significant trauma work in previous therapy. This helped her move to a place of recognition of the reality of her gender dysphoria. Even as she did trauma work, she found that her gender dysphoria persisted. She came to see that she experienced great shame around her gender identity, and gender dysphoria was a barrier to living in her body that complicated her process of eating-disorder recovery immensely. In light of this, she was motivated to forge a pathway for herself forward, although she was terrified at where she might go from here.

PHASE FOUR: CONSOLIDATING GENDER IDENTITY

The final phase of therapy involved helping Rae explore gender identity without a fixed outcome. She began to identify situations and experiences that heighten gender dysphoria, such as during her period, which was returning predictably as she addressed her disordered eating and regularly nourished her body. She was able to track her period and buffer against this distress by planning to increase connection with others around that time, to use mindfulness skills to stay grounded, and to shift attention away from the distress through distraction with planned meaningful activities. She also practiced adaptive coping skills as she managed gender-related distress from day to day. She came to realize that, with her bipolar symptoms managed more effectively, the intensity of her gender dysphoria was less overpowering to her than it had ever been before.

Rae began reading various resources and stories of other people who experienced gender dysphoria and specifically was drawn to the idea of gender fluidity as a helpful concept for her. She recognized that she never had permission to figure out what presentation felt consistent with her gender identity given how her mother hyperfocused on rigid stereotypes as a guide for dress. She realized that her adopting a more gender-neutral presentation in high school was in part a reaction to her mother's rigidity and an act of rebellion against her upbringing. As she realized this, she shifted focus away from considering use of hormonal therapy or potential surgeries and began to adopt, through trial and error, various presentations that allowed for increased comfort. She was struck by her recognition that, as her mood symptoms remained stable, she began to miss wearing makeup some days. She shifted her dress, style, and makeup from day to day and found that this newfound flexibility worked for her.

Rae also reported that as she maintained nourishment, she was able to adjust to her body with greater ease and reduced anxiety. She continued to struggle with body-image acceptance at times. When this was heightened, she validated and soothed emotional pain with skills she was learning in therapy.

FINAL REFLECTIONS

Rae's is a story of yet another possible way of managing gender-dysphoria conflicts. At the end of therapy she reported increasing connectedness to her body, improved mood stability and mental clarity as a result of medication management and therapy around co-occurring symptoms, increased capacity to disrupt restrictive eating habits, and adoption of a presentation that shifted based on her level of gender dysphoria. In terms of finding her current plateau, Rae chose not to adopt a gender-identity label, continuing to use her birth name and female pronouns, and reported little discomfort with this on most days. She actively challenged rigid stereotypes when she was confronted with them and used self-talk to comfort herself when these stereotypes triggered feelings of shame. She found ways to connect to her body through mindful movement that felt less threatening to her, but she continued at times to experience gender-related distress. She found strategies to cope with this that allowed her to live in her body, recognizing that the intensity of gender dysphoria could continue to ebb and flow in intensity over time. She identified boundaries she could set with her family of origin regarding the comments they would sometimes make about her presentation and practiced assertive responses that increased her sense of empowerment. She moved to a place of greater self-acceptance, improved self-worth, reduced shame around gender identity, and insight into the complicating factors in this process.

REFERENCES

American Psychiatric Association. (2013). *Diagnostic and statistical manual of mental disorders: DSM-5* (5th ed.).

American Psychological Association. (2010). Ethical principles of psychologists and code of conduct. www.apa.org/ethics/code/principles.pdf.

American Psychological Association. (2015). Guidelines for psychological practice with transgender and gender nonconforming people. *American Psychologist, 70*(9), 832-64. doi:10.1037/a0039906

American Psychological Association, Task Force on Gender Identity and Gender Variance. (2009). *Report of the task force on gender identity and gender variance.* www.apa.org/pi/lgbt/resources/policy/gender-identity-report.pdf

Berg, D., & Edwards-Leeper, L. (2018). Child and family assessment. In C. Keo-Meier & D. Ehrensaft (Eds.), *The gender affirmative model: An interdisciplinary approach to supportive transgender and gender expansive children* (pp. 101-24). American Psychological Association.

Boghani, P. (Reporter and producer). (2015, June 30). When transgender kids transition, medical risks are both known and unknown [Television series episode]. *Frontline.* PBS. https://www.pbs.org/wgbh/frontline/article/when-transgender-kids-transition-medical-risks-are-both-known-and-unknown/

Cantor, J. (2018, October 17). American Academy of Pediatrics policy and trans-kids: Fact-checking [Web log post]. Sexology Today! www.sexologytoday.org/2018/10/american-academy-of-pediatrics-policy.html

Chen, D., Edwards-Leeper, L., Stancin, T., & Tishelman, A. (2018). Advancing the practice of pediatric psychology with transgender youth: State of the science, ongoing controversies, and future directions. *Clinical Practice in Pediatric Psychology, 6*(1), 73-83. doi:10.1037/cpp0000229

Cochran, B. N., Reed, O. M., & Gleason, H. A. (2018). Providing a welcoming clinical environment. In M. R. Kauth & J. C. Shipherd (Eds.), *Adult transgender care: An interdisciplinary approach for training mental health professionals* (pp. 44-60). Routledge.

Coleman, E., Bockting, W., Botzer, M., Cohen-Kettenis, P., DeCuypere, G., Feldman, J., Fraser, L., Green, J., Knudson, G., Meyer, W. J., Monstrey, S., Adler, R. K., Brown, G. R., Devor, A. H., Ehrbar, R., Ettner, R., Eyler, E., Garofalo, R., Karasic, D. H., . . . Zucker, K. (2012). *WPATH standards of care for the health of transsexual, transgender, and gender non-conforming people* (7th ed.). World Professional Association for Transgender Health.

Cox, C. (2021, April 8). As Arkansas bans treatments for transgender youth, 15 other states consider similar bills. *USA Today.* www.usatoday.com/story/news/politics/2021/04/08 /states-consider-bills-medical-treatments-transgender-youth/7129101002/

Doward, J. (2018, November 3). Gender identity clinic accused of fast-tracking young adults. *The Observer.* www.theguardian.com/society/2018/nov/03/tavistock-centre -gender-identity-clinic-accused-fast-tracking-young-adults

Edwards-Leeper, L., Leibowitz, S., & Sangganjanavanich, V. F. (2016). Affirmative practice with transgender and gender nonconforming youth: Expanding the model. *Psychology of Sexual Orientation and Gender Diversity, 3*(2), 165-72. doi:10.1037/sgd0000167

Ehrensaft, D. (2018). Exploring gender expansive expressions. In C. Keo-Meier & D. Ehrensaft (Eds.), *The gender affirmative model: An interdisciplinary approach to supporting transgender and gender expansive children* (pp. 37-53). American Psychological Association.

Firek, A. F., & Sawan-Garcia, R. (2018). Preparing clients for hormone therapy. In M. R. Kauth & J. C. Shipherd (Eds.), *Adult transgender care: an interdisciplinary approach for training mental health professionals* (pp. 78-100). Routledge.

Flores, A. F., Brown, T. N. T., & Herman, J. L. (2016, October). *Race and ethnicity of adults who identify as transgender in the United States.* The Williams Institute.

Gagnon, R. A. J. (2007). Transsexuality and ordination. www.robgagnon.net/articles /TranssexualityOrdination.pdf

Glaser, C. (Ed.). (2008). *Gender identity and our faith communities: A congregational guide to transgender advocacy.* Human Rights Campaign Foundation. https://assets2.hrc .org/files/assets/resources/Gender-Identity-and-our-Faith-Communities_2008-12.pdf

Hacking, I. (1995). The looping effects of human kinds. In Dan Sperber, David Premack, & Ann James Premack (Eds.), *Causal Cognition A Multidisciplinary Debate* (p. 368). University of Oxford Press.

Hall, T. W., Tisdale, T. C., & Brokaw, B. F. (1994). Assessment of religious dimensions in Christian clients: A review of selected instruments for research and clinical use. *Journal of Psychology and Theology, 22*(4), 395-421.

Hathaway, W. L., Scott, S. Y., & Garver, S. A. (2004). Assessing religious/spiritual functioning: A neglected domain in clinical practice? *Professional Psychology: Research and Practice, 35*(1), 97-104.

Hendricks, M. L., & Testa, R. J. (2012). A conceptual framework for clinical work with transgender and gender nonconforming clients: An adaptation of the Minority Stress Model. *Professional Psychology: Research and Practice, 43*(5), 460-67. http://doi.org /10.1037/a0029597

Hodge, D. R. (2001). Spiritual genograms: A generational approach to assessing spirituality. *Families in Society: The Journal of Contemporary Human Services, 82*(1), 35-48.

Hook, J. N., Worthington, E. L. Jr., Davis, D. E., Jennings, D. J. II, Gartner, A. L., & Hook, J. P. (2010). Empirically supported religious and spiritual therapies. *Journal of Clinical Psychology, 66*(1), 46-72.

Hopwood, R. A., & Witten, T. M. (2017). Spirituality, faith, and religion: The TGNC experience. In A. A. Singh & l. m. dickey (Eds.), *Affirmative counseling and psychological practice with transgender and gender nonconforming clients* (pp. 225-26). American Psychological Association.

James, S. E., Herman, J. L., Rankin, S., Keisling, M., Mottet, L., & Anafi, M. (2016). *The report of the 2015 U.S. transgender survey.* National Center for Transgender Equality. www.ustranssurvey.org

Katz-Wise, S. L., Rosario, M., & Tsappis, M. (2016). Lesbian, gay, bisexual, and transgender youth and family acceptance, *Pediatric Clinics of North America 63*(6), 1011-25.

Kauth, M. R., & Shipherd, J. C. (Eds.). (2018). *Adult transgender care: An interdisciplinary approach for training mental health professionals.* Routledge.

Lamb, K. (2020, February 6). National firestorm on horizon as states consider criminalizing transgender treatments for youth. *USA Today.* www.usatoday.com/story/news/nation /2020/02/06/transgender-youth-transition-treatment-state-bills/4605054002/

Leef, J. H., Brian, J., VanderLaan, D. P., Wood, H., Scott, K., Lai, M.-C., Bradley, S. J., & Zucker, K. J. (2019). Traits of autism spectrum disorder in school-aged children with gender dysphoria: A comparison to clinical controls. *Clinical Practice in Pediatric Psychology, 7*(4), 383-95. http://doi.org/10.1037/cpp0000303

McAdams, D. P. (2014). Personal narratives and the life story. In O. P. John, R. W. Robins, & L. A. Pervin (Eds.), *Handbook of personality: Theory and research* (3rd ed.) (pp. 242-62). Guilford.

McAdams, D. P. (2001). The psychology of life stories. *Review of General Psychology, 5*(2), 100-122.

Morgan, A. (2000). *What is narrative therapy?: An easy-to-read introduction.* Dulwich Centre.

Moriarty, G. L. & Hoffman, L. (Eds.). (2014). *God image handbook for spiritual counseling and psychotherapy: Research, theory, and practice.* Haworth Pastoral Press.

Porter, K. E., Ronneberg, C. R., & Witten, T. M. (2013). Religious affiliation and successful aging among transgender older adults: Findings from the Trans MetLife Survey. *Journal of Religion, Spirituality & Aging, 25*(2), 112-38.

Rafferty, J., Committee on Psychosocial Aspects of Child and Family Health, Committee on Adolescence, & Section on Lesbian, Gay, Bisexual, and Transgender Health and Wellness. (2018). Ensuring comprehensive care and support for transgender and gender-diverse children and adolescents. *Pediatrics, 142*(4). https://pediatrics.aappub lications.org/content/142/4/e20182162

Ruttimann, J. (2013, January). Blocking puberty in transgender youth. *Endocrine News.* https://endocrinenews.endocrine.org/blocking-puberty-in-transgender-youth/

Sadusky, J., & Yarhouse, M. A. (2020). Cultural humility & gender identity. *Reflections, 26*(2), 107-13.

Sells, J. N., & Yarhouse, M. A. (2011). *Counseling couples in conflict: A relational restoration model.* IVP Academic.

Singh, A. A. (2013). Transgender youth of color and resilience: Negotiating oppression and finding support. *Sex Roles, 68,* 690-702. http://dx.doi.org/10.1007/s11199-012-0149-z

Sloan, C. A., & Berke, D. S. (2018). Dialectical behavioral therapy as a treatment option for complex cases of gender dysphoria. In M. R. Kauth & J. C. Shipherd (Eds.), *Adult transgender care: An interdisciplinary approach for training mental health professionals* (pp. 123-39). Routledge.

Sloan, C. A., & Safer J. D. (2018). The high-risk client: Comorbid conditions that affect care. In M. R. Kauth & J. C. Shipherd (Eds.), *Adult transgender care: An interdisciplinary approach for training mental health professionals* (pp. 101-22). Routledge.

Smith, T. B., Bartz, J., & Richards, P. S. (2007). Outcomes of religious and spiritual adaptations in psychotherapy: A meta-analytic review. *Psychotherapy Research, 17*(6), 643-55.

Steensma, T. D., Biemond, R., de Boer, F., & Cohen-Kettenis, P. T. (2011). Desisting and persisting gender dysphoria after childhood: A qualitative follow-up study. *Clinical Child Psychology and Psychiatry, 16*(4), 499-516.

Strang, J. F., Meagher, H., Kenworthy, L., de Vries, A. L. C., Menvielle, E., Leibowitz, S., Janssen, A., Cohen-Kettenis, P., Shumer, D. E., Edwards-Leeper, L., Pleak, R. R., Spack, N., Karasic, D. H., Schreier, H., Balleur, A., Tishelman, A., Ehrensaft, D., Rodnan, L., Kuschner, E. S., . . . Anthony, L. G. (2018). Initial clinical guidelines for co-occurring autism spectrum disorder and gender dysphoria or incongruence in adolescents. *Journal of Clinical Child & Adolescent Psychology, 47*(1), 105-15. https://doi.org/10.108 0/15374416.2016.1228462

Substance Abuse and Mental Health Services Administration. (2015). Ending conversion therapy: Supporting and affirming LGBTQ youth. HHS Publication SMA15-4928.

Vogel, D. L., Bitman, R. L., Hammer, J. H., & Wade, N. G. (2013). Is stigma internalized?: The longitudinal impact of public stigma on self-stigma. *Journal of Counseling Psychology, 60*(2), 311-16.

Ward, D. J. (2011). The lived experience of spiritual abuse. *Mental Health, Religion & Culture, 14*(9), 899-915.

Weinand, J. D., & Safer, J. D. (2015). Hormone therapy in transgender adults is safe with provider supervision: A review of hormone therapy sequelae for transgender individuals. *Journal of Clinical and Translational Endocrinology, 2*(2), 55-60.

Xavier, J. M. (2000). *The Washington, DC, transgender needs assessment survey.* Us Helping Us—People into Living. www.glaa.org/archive/2000/tgneedsassessment1112.shtml

Yarhouse, M. A. (2015). *Understanding gender dysphoria: Navigating transgender issues in a changing culture.* InterVarsity Press.

Yarhouse, M. A. (2010). *Homosexuality and the Christian: A guide for parents, pastors, and friends*. BethanyHouse.

Yarhouse, M. A., Carr, T. L., Bucher, E. K. & Cruise, C. (2020). *Gender identity journeys: A workbook for navigating gender dysphoria*. Wheaton College: Sexual & Gender Identity Institute.

Yarhouse, M. A., & Houp, D. (2016). Transgender Christians: Gender identity, family relationships, and religious faith. In Sheyma Vaughn (Ed.), *Transgender youth: Perceptions, media influences, and social challenges* (pp. 51-65). Nova Science Publishers.

Yarhouse, M. A., & Sadusky, J. (2020). *Emerging gender identities: Understanding the diverse experiences of today's youth*. Brazos Press.

Yarhouse, M. A., & Zaporozhets, O. (in press). *When children come out*. IVP Academic.

Zraick, K. (2019, November 28). Texas father says seven-year-old isn't transgender, igniting a politicized outcry. *New York Times*. www.nytimes.com/2019/10/28/us/texas-transgender-child.html

Zucker, K. J. (2020a). Debate: Different strokes for different folks. *Child and Adolescent Mental Health, 25*(1), 36-37.

Zucker, K. J. (2020b). Gender dysphoria in children and adolescents. In K. S. K. Hall & Y. M. Binik (Eds.), *Principles and practices of sex therapy* (6th ed.) (pp. 395-422). Guilford Press.

INDEX

CAPS

_An Association for Christian Psychologists,
Therapists, Counselors and Academicians_

CAPS is a vibrant Christian organization with a rich tradition. Founded in 1956 by a small group of Christian mental health professionals, chaplains and pastors, CAPS has grown to more than 2,100 members in the U.S., Canada and more than 25 other countries.

CAPS encourages in-depth consideration of therapeutic, research, theoretical and theological issues. The association is a forum for creative new ideas. In fact, their publications and conferences are the birthplace for many of the formative concepts in our field today.

CAPS members represent a variety of denominations, professional groups and theoretical orientations; yet all are united in their commitment to Christ and to professional excellence.

CAPS is a non-profit, member-supported organization. It is led by a fully functioning board of directors, and the membership has a voice in the direction of CAPS.

CAPS is more than a professional association. It is a fellowship, and in addition to national and international activities, the organization strongly encourages regional, local and area activities which provide networking and fellowship opportunities as well as professional enrichment.

To learn more about CAPS, visit www.caps.net.

CAPS BOOKS
from IVP Academic

The joint publishing venture between IVP Academic and CAPS aims to promote the understanding of the relationship between Christianity and the behavioral sciences at both the clinical/counseling and the theoretical/research levels. These books will be of particular value for students and practitioners, teachers and researchers.

For more information about CAPS Books, visit InterVarsity Press's website at www.ivpress.com/christian-association-for-psychological-studies-books-set.

ALSO BY
MARK YARHOUSE

**Understanding
Gender Dysphoria**
978-0-8308-2859-3

Sexuality and Sex Therapy
978-0-8308-2853-1

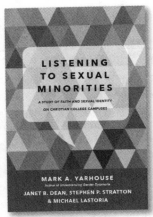

Listening to Sexual Minorities
978-0-8308-2862-3

Family Therapies
978-0-8308-2854-8